A MODERN JONAH MIDRASH & COMMENTARY

A midrash written using Ancient Bible Study Methods - Updated

Michael Koplitz

Michael Hivner

Table of Contents

ACKNOWLEDGMENTS

Mr. Michael Hivner and I studied the book of Jonah after I wrote the Jonah Commentary using Ancient Bible Study Methods. We saw how many details were not in the story. When we were finished, I had the idea of taking our observations and thoughts and writing a Jonah Midrash story. The Midrash fills in a lot of the details that are not a part of the original biblical story. It is hoped that the Midrash will make the story of Jonah more real to the reader.

"Midrash is an interpretive act, seeking the answers to religious questions (both practical and theological) by plumbing the meaning of the words of the <u>Torah.</u> (In the <u>Bible</u>, the root d-r-sh is used to mean inquiring into any matter, including occasionally to seek God's word.) Midrash responds to contemporary problems and crafts new stories, making connections between new Jewish realities and the unchanging biblical text."[1]

---

[1] https://www.myjewishlearning.com/article/midrash-101. Accessed December 18, 2017.

A Modern-Day Midrash of the book of Jonah

Chapter 1

Greetings in the name of the LORD God of Israel, the God of Abraham, the God of Isaac and the God of Jacob. My name is Jonah, son of Amittai. I had an exciting adventure that I would like to tell you about. It all started one beautiful spring day when I went out of my house to feed the animals on the farm. After I was done feeding the animals, I decided to sit back and relax. Much to my surprise the word of the LORD God came to me, "go at once to Nineveh, that great city, and cry out against it; for their wickedness has come up before me." Of course, at first, I was stunned. Why would the LORD God speak to me a lonely farmer? I was nobody important, at least I thought so. I had grown up in my small town in the Northern Kingdom of Israel. I learned my Torah and about our God of the Mountain of Sinai. I did not have any advanced training because my teacher saw nothing unusual in me for more Torah study. For some reason the LORD God, saw something in me that day and wanted me to do something for Him.

But to go to Nineveh, that was asking a bit too much. The Ninevites who lived north of us had created a large army. They were invading the territories of the nations of the north and we feared that one day they would turn their eyes upon us. Several of our traveling caravans of merchants were seized by the Ninevites, robbed and killed. I was taught that you can never trust the Ninevites. So, why in the world would the LORD God want me to go to Nineveh and cry out against it for all the wickedness that they were doing? It would be better for the LORD God destroyed us if. Also, I never traveled outside the boundaries of the Northern Kingdom. I had no experience, no knowledge, and no wealth to make such a journey.

That evening I went to sleep tired from the day's work. I had a dream that evening, and in that dream the LORD God spoke to me again, telling me I needed to go to Nineveh, that great city, and cry out against it because of its wickedness. The dream woke me up, and it was near daybreak so, I got out of bed and decided that I needed to get away from the LORD God because I felt He would not stop telling me to go to the Ninevites. I was taught that the LORD God of Israel remained within the borders of the Promised Land. So, I figured I could leave the country and go somewhere else, then the LORD God could not find me and force me to go to Nineveh. In the back of my mind, I knew I was disobeying the LORD God. But this trip to Nineveh scared me more than my fear for the LORD God.

But where would I go? I decided I would go to the furthest city away from the Northern Kingdom of Israel. I would go to the town of Tarshish. The fastest way to get to Tarshish and away from my home was to get passage on a ship that was heading in that direction. So, I went down to Joppa in search of finding a boat. I brought all the money that I had, and I was fortunate because it was just enough to pay for my fare with a little leftover. I got on board the ship, hoping that I could get away from the presence of the LORD God. I did not have any luggage with me, not even a change in clothes. Frankly, it was just me. Luckily for me, none of the sailors on the boat asked me why I was going to Tarshish without a change of clothing.

The sea was calm as we left from Joppa. It was a beautiful spring day, and the warm breeze off the sea felt wonderful upon my face. We had been at sea for two days when a great wind came upon the sea, and a mighty storm raged toward us. The captain told us he had never seen a rainstorm so intense. I could see in the captain's face that he was afraid that the wind would capsize the boat. The storm forced us to move away from the shoreline. After a time, you could not see the coastline anymore. We did not know where we were.

I realized this storm must have been from the LORD God. Since this was a storm, the captain had never seen, and because of its intensity, it had to be from the Spirit of God. The first thing

I realized is that the LORD God was not contained to just the Promised Land. The LORD God is the ruler and creator of the Earth and all that was in it. I became terrified to the point where I could not do anything. Therefore, I sat down on the deck near a mast and held on as tightly as I could. The boat was rocking back-and-forth and up and down, which made it almost impossible to hold on to the mast. But I held on because I knew that if I let go I would have been thrown into the sea and lost forever. To make sure that I was not thrown into the sea, I managed to walk down the stairs into the hold of the boat. I figured that the LORD God had sent the storm to kill me. So, I laid on the deck, curled up, and was prepared to die. I fell asleep believing that I would never wake up again.

The sailors were afraid that they were going to die, so each of them cried out to their own god. But nothing changed, and the storm continued to intensify. Thus, the sailors threw the cargo that was on the ship into the sea, hoping that the lighter boat would survive. The first cargo they threw overboard was their metal and wooden idols. They prayed hard to those idols, and nothing happened. They had lost confidence in their false gods and threw them into the sea. Perhaps they thought a stronger God than theirs brought this storm upon them. When the rain did not stop, they threw the rest of the cargo on the ship into the sea. Yet the storm raged on.

The captain of the ship came down into the hold of the boat to find me asleep. He yelled at me, which woke me up. The captain said to me, "How can you be asleep?" The captain told me that the storm had intensified and that they prayed to each of their gods and nothing happened. The captain thought that perhaps if I prayed to my God, the creator of heaven and earth, that I might get the storm to pass to save the boat and the sailors that were on it. So, I prayed to the LORD God, and I said to him that the ship and the people on board the vessel should be spared because it was I, Jonah, who had run away from the LORD God and it is I who should be punished. I asked the LORD God to spare those who were with me. But the storm raged on.

Since the storm did not subside, the sailors said to one another, "Come, let us cast lots, so that we may know on whose account this calamity has come upon us." I knew that the calamity of the storm was my fault and probably should have come out and said so, but I did not. Thus, the sailors cast their lots, and four out of the five lots landed on me. The sailors looked at me and said, "Tell us why this calamity has come upon us? What is your occupation? Where do you come from? What is your country? And what people are you?"

I told them I was a Hebrew from the Northern Kingdom of Israel and that I worship the one and true God who is the creator of heaven and earth. I was astonished that these men became more afraid. They must have known something about the LORD God of the Hebrew people. They looked at me and asked me why I was fleeing the presence of my LORD God. I had told them that the purpose of my trip was to flee from the presence of my LORD God when I boarded the boat. Most of them mocked me and some of them even laughed at me. Well, they were not laughing anymore.

Now they were scared and frightened.

I knew in my heart that the LORD God was coming after me and that the only way to save the men on the boat was to have them throw me overboard. So, I offered a prayer to my LORD God and said, "LORD God, it was wrong of me to run away from you. Please spare these men because they had nothing to do with my disobedience. LORD, God forgive me for trying to run away from your presence." Then I looked at the sailors and said to them they needed to throw me into the sea and that the sea would quiet down because the LORD God was only interested in me. I told them that the LORD God was a compassionate and gracious God and would not take vengeance on them, for they did not know what they were doing when they took me on board to give me passage to the city of Tarshish.

The sailors did not throw me overboard. They either did not believe my story, or they were so compassionate that they did not want me to die. Each man got to an ore of the boat and started rowing to shore. They rowed faster and faster to make it to the shoreline. But the harder they rowed, the further away from the coastline we traveled. The storm was getting worse when finally; they consented to my request, and they threw me overboard.

The sailors on the boat, led by the captain, cried out to the LORD God, and asked the LORD God to spare their lives and not hold them personally accountable for my death. I told them that the LORD God was merciful and that He would not hold them responsible for my death. I knew it was my responsibility and that it was my actions that brought on the storm. I knew that my disobedience by running away from the LORD God required a punishment. The men on the boat did not commit any crime when they threw me overboard and must not be punished.

I could tell that these men knew the God of Israel. After they threw me overboard, the storm subsided, and they could row to the shoreline. They disembarked and traveled into the town to purchase a lamb. They brought the lamb back to the seashore and offered it as a sacrifice to the LORD God. They also took a vow that the God of Israel would now be their God. Therefore, something good happened out of my disobedience. I could bring nine men into the presence of the LORD God. This also taught me that the God of Israel not only lived everywhere in the world but that the God of Israel was indeed the God of all people because these nine men who did not know the LORD God became believers and follower.

I was in the ocean, bobbing up and down. I was trying to save my life, but I was not sure how that was going to happen because I was a long way from the shoreline, and I did not have a boat to take me to it. A loud noise that was behind me startled me. I could turn around and saw a large fish coming toward me. I had never seen a fish this large before in my entire life.

The giant fish opened its mouth, and its gullet was large enough to swallow me whole. That is precisely what happened. The giant fish swallowed me, and I landed in the fish's belly. I knew that what I did was wrong, but did the LORD God have to punish me in this way? I could never see my family again. I could never read from God's Torah again. I could never go back and visit the magnificent Temple in Jerusalem, which was sanctified to the LORD God ever again. So, for three days and three nights, I sat in the belly of this giant fish with no idea what was going to happen next. The air was foul. I was thirsty and hungry. I wondered what the LORD God had in store for me now.

Chapter 2

So, I found myself inside the belly of a large fish. Being swallowed by the fish was an interesting experience, one that I hope I will never have to repeat. It was extremely dark inside the belly of the fish. I tried to walk around but it was difficult because I sank into the stomach of the fish every time I tried to move. I wondered how I was going to get out of this fish before I died. I wondered how long someone could live in such a situation.

I looked down and I could see that I was standing in water and there were a lot of fish swimming around. I noticed that one of the fish glowed and was giving off light. I waited until that fish came near my leg and I grabbed and pulled it out of the water. The fish squirmed and tried to get out of my hands, so it could jump back into the water and as it squirmed, I made my grip tighter. I took the fish and used it like a lantern. The glow from the fish was bright enough that I could see one of the walls of the stomach. I walked toward the wall and put my hand on it and found it to be quite fleshy.

I looked up, held the fish up, and I could see an opening just above me. That had to be the gullet of the fish. But how was I going to get up there? I tried to climb up the walls of the stomach, but there was nowhere to grip it. I tried to climb up the wall using my bare hands, but that worked neither. Then I heard an awful noise, and a rush of water came down from the opening above me.

The water landed upon my head, and I could feel different fish bouncing off from my scalp. It was not a pleasant experience.

This place must be like being in Sheol. If this was truly like Sheol, I wondered if the LORD God could hear me. So, I cried out from the depths of the belly of the fish to my LORD God. I said, "For you had cast me into the deep, into the heart of the seas, and the current engulfed me. All your breakers and billows passed over me. Lord God, I have been expelled from your sight. I will look again toward your holy Temple."

But how was I going to know if God heard my cry? I was away from the land of Israel. I was far away from the Temple in Jerusalem where the LORD God lives. How could the LORD God hear me when I was so far away from my homeland? But then I remember the promises that the LORD God had made to my ancestor Abraham, and I said to myself that I am one of God's chosen people. He cannot let me die this way. So, I prayed to the Lord, and I asked for his forgiveness. I should have trusted the LORD God because he knows everything. How wrong was it for me to take it upon myself that I would know better than the LORD God. I knew I had little time left before I would die in the fish's belly. I would not throw myself onto the "ground" and pray but that would put me in the water and surely, I would die. As I was standing, I prayed to the LORD God and asked that He would have mercy upon me and that if He would save me, I will do whatever He commands.

I thought about the sailors who were on the ship with me and how they regarded their vain idols. I said to the LORD God, "Why did you not take some sailors from the ship? After all, they were idol worshipers and I am a worshiper of you, LORD God, Lord of all. Why is it I get punished but they did not? I am the one who has served you, LORD God, and praised your holy name. Okay, this one time I disobeyed a direct order from you, LORD God. But does not it count that I have been loyal to you in so many ways? I have kept all the commandments of the Torah. I have attended every Shabbat service. I celebrate the feasts and prayers on the holiest of days. Why are you going to let me die with these other fish?

LORD God, I know that salvation only comes from you and if you let me live, I will go to Nineveh and I will preach your word there. I will go to Nineveh and bring them the message that you wanted me to before being eaten by this large fish. The LORD God heard my cry and my prayer of confession. And in the goodness of the LORD God's heart, felt compelled to give me forgiveness and to give him one more chance.

Unbeknownst to me, the large fish could travel quickly. In three days, the fish swam from the Mediterranean Sea all the way to the Persian Gulf and when the fish reached the beaches of Babylon, it quivered. I wondered what was about to happen because I could feel the stomach walls quaking and quivering. Did the big fish eat something bad? I was not sure what was happening. Suddenly, I could see a light entering the belly from outside, which meant that the fish must have opened its mouth wide. With one final quivering thrust, I was vomited out of the fish. Even though it was rather disgusting to have been vomited with half-digested fish, I sat on the ground at the edge of the water and immediately gave thanks to the LORD God for saving my life.

Chapter 3

I found myself near the mouth of the Euphrates River, which empties into the Persian Gulf. I knew that the water in the Euphrates River was salt free, therefore I walked into the river with my clothes on. I knew I needed to get cleaned up, and I knew that my clothing stunk of fish. The waters of the Euphrates River were nice and warm, and it really felt good to get clean. I was also very thirsty as I had had nothing to drink or eat for the last three days. I put my hand into the Euphrates and drew up some water to drink. It felt so good to drink and to see the sun again. It took a few minutes for my eyes to get adjusted. I was in one piece.

I sat down on the ground and fell asleep. After being awake for three days, I really needed the sleep. I do not know how long I was sleeping, but then I heard a voice calling out my name. I woke up, and I looked around and I did not see anyone there. So, I closed my eyes and tried to fall back asleep. But then I heard the voice again calling my name "Jonah, Jonah." But this time I called out, "Is that you, LORD God calling me?"

It was certainly the LORD God calling out to me. The LORD GOD reminded me of the promise that I had made while I was in the fish's belly, that I would do and go wherever the LORD God was about to send me. Then I heard the LORD God say, "Arise, go to Nineveh, the great city and proclaim to it the proclamation which I am going to give you." I was not thrilled to take this message from the LORD God. I thought the LORD God would have figured out from the first time that I did not want to go into the city of Nineveh and certainly not proclaim the possibility of salvation for such a wicked people on earth. However, I remembered what I said to the LORD God inside the stomach of the fish and remember that I said I would do anything that the LORD God commanded me to do.

So, I needed to walk to Nineveh. The city was at least a three-day trip, and I did not have any supplies. I had eaten nothing in three days and had nothing to drink except what I had at the Euphrates River. Luckily, there was a small town about 250 feet ahead of me. I walked over to the small town, and I asked a local person, "Where can I buy some food?" The local person was very kind to me and directed me to the marketplace. Luckily for me, I had some money left after I bought the boat in Joppa. I could buy several days of food and water. While I was in the marketplace, I even had a sandwich. I realized that the food in the marketplace was not kosher, but when you have been in the fish's belly for three days and you are that hungry, anything works.

I approached the city gates of Nineveh, where I was greeted by several people. I was an outsider since I was dressed in different clothing than what the people were wearing. However, they were very kind to me and invited me into the city and offered me a tour. I told them that the LORD God, the creator of heaven and earth, had sent me to bring them a warning that the LORD God would overthrow because of all her sins. I told them the LORD God sent me to tell the people that they must change their ways before God's judgment became final.

At first, they did not believe me and several of the people wanted to throw me out of the city. So, I explained to them what happened to me, that I was in the belly of the big fish for three days. I did not have food or water, yet the LORD God kept me alive, and the large fish spit me out because I agreed to come to Nineveh and to bring this information to the people of Nineveh so that they would not be destroyed.

People asked me what they needed to do. I told them they needed to change from their evil ways and to stop sinning. I told them they should come together for a time of mourning and that they must wear sackcloth so that the LORD God could see that they were truly repenting of their sins. I was quite surprised that the people listened to me. They ran into their homes, and they came out wearing sackcloth. They knocked on the doors of other houses to tell people they needed to put on sackcloth and that it was time for Nineveh to rid itself of its sinful ways.

When the word reached the king, I became scared again because kings dislike to be told by prophets of the LORD God what should and should not happen. The king, upon hearing what I had said, rose from his throne, took off his robes, and put on sackcloth. The king decreed a proclamation that went out throughout the city to all the noblemen and to the common people that everyone was too fast for the next day and that everyone must be covered in sackcloth. Even the animals must be covered with sackcloth. The city of Nineveh observed a day of mourning, and each person was told to pray to the LORD God that he would forgive them for their sins and help them turn away from their wrongdoing.

The King proclaimed, "who knows, God may withdraw his burning anger so that we will not perish." All the people of the city of Nineveh, in their sackcloth, dropped to their knees, and you could hear all the people doing this at the same time all the way to Jerusalem. The people cried out to the LORD God to forgive them for what they had done.

When the LORD God saw their deeds, that they had turned away from their wicked ways, the LORD God relented concerning the calamity which he had planned to bring upon them and he did not punish them. Not only did the people of Nineveh change their minds, but that it was also possible to change the LORD God's mind. Oh, I wished that my people back in the northern kingdom of Israel would do the same thing that the people of Nineveh had done today.

Chapter 4

I thought about my people who refused to obey the laws of the LORD God. We had received his commandments and his Torah. We received the Promised Land that He had promised to our father Abraham. He took us out of the clutches of slavery in Egypt and offered us salvation at Mount Sinai. But over the years, we have turned to sin. We were not as wicked as the people of Nineveh. However, sin was in my country.

I felt like a traitor to my people. For many years, groups of Ninevites soldiers would attack our northern border. They would steal our food and rape our women. Our army was not strong enough to fight off the Ninevites. Yet here I was in the city of Nineveh, saving it from the wrath of the LORD God. The more I thought about what God had me do, the more displeased and angry I became? I am not sure whether I was angry at myself, at the LORD God, or at my people.

I tried to avoid taking the message of salvation to our enemies in Nineveh. The LORD God wanted this to be done and sent a large fish after me. After being in the belly of that large fish for three days, I had to do what LORD God said or die in that fish. But every time I thought about it, I got angrier. So, I prayed to the LORD God and asked him if He would take my life. I did not deserve to live because I felt like such a traitor to my people. I know I was serving the LORD God, but I just couldn't help feeling this way. I believed that death was better for me than to continue to live a life as a traitor.

It was a long way back to the Northern Kingdom of Israel so; I decided that since evening was upon me, I would stay at Nineveh. I went outside the eastern gate of the city and set up a shelter for myself so that I could get some sleep that night. As I was sleeping, I heard a voice call out my name, "Jonah, Jonah." This time I knew it was the LORD God calling my name so, I answered, and the LORD God said to me, "Do you have good reason to be angry?"

I decided I was going to stay in my shelter, even if it took several days to see what was going to happen to the city of Nineveh. Perhaps, after a day or so, they would go back to their evil ways and the LORD God would strike them down like he did to Sodom and Gomorrah. During that evening, the LORD God anointed a plant, and it grew up over me and became a shade over my head. An easterly wind had blown that night, and it took off the roof of the shelter that I had built. If it was not for the plant that the LORD God had given to me, the night would have been uncomfortable. I was happy with that plant.

As the sun rose in the east that morning, I was surprised to see that a worm had come and attack the plant, and it had withered and died. When the sun had come up. The LORD God appointed a scorching heat, and the sun to beat down on my head so that I became faint. It was so hot that I begged the LORD God to let me die, for death was better than this life that I had.

I became furious that I lost this plant that the LORD God had given to me and I felt I had a very good reason to ask the LORD God to take my life now because it would end the pain-and-suffering that I was going through. Again, I heard the LORD God calling out my name, and He said, "You had compassion on the plant for which you did not work in which you did not cause to grow, which came up overnight and perished overnight. Should I the LORD God, not have compassion on the city of Nineveh, the great city in which there are over 120,000 persons? They did not know the difference between the right and left hand?"

I wondered what the Lord was talking about and as I thought about it the thought occurred to me that the LORD God was teaching me another lesson. The first lesson came in the belly of the large fish when I tried to run away from the commands of the LORD God. I learned that if the LORD God speaks to me I need to listen and to obey because He is the creator of heaven and earth and all that I am and all that I have is because of Him. I must always show thanksgiving to the LORD God because He is always good and just. The LORD God is the God of all people, not just the Hebrews living in the promised land.

The second lesson was about the plant. The plants and the animals of the earth belong to the LORD God. Indeed, even people belong to the LORD God, for the Torah tells us that the LORD God made us in His image. Therefore, I learned that if the LORD God wants to save a group of people, like the Ninevites, it is not my place to ask why, or how, but rather to accept the will of the LORD God.

The third lesson is that I shouldn't be upset that these foreigners, the Ninevites, responded to the warning of the LORD God to change their ways and that he offered them salvation. For they had the free choice to say yes or no. My countrymen back in the kingdom of Israel have the choice to determine if they are going to follow the word of the LORD God which was brought to them through Moses and the prophets or were they going to reject the LORD God and continue their sinful ways. If they continue in their sinful ways, one day, the Lord God will punish them in the same way He intended to punish the Ninevites.

Introduction to the Commentary

While I was attending Seminary earning my M. Div. degree, I questioned what the instructors and reference books, which were required, were saying about the Scriptures. One idea being offered then was that the Bible was full of errors and not factual. I found that attitude disturbing for seminary instructors to be teaching. After all, the Seminary experience is to train pastors to go out into God's world and preach the Bible. How can you preach the Bible if you believe what these instructors are teaching? The methods that were being taught to examine the Bible just seemed inaccurate to me.

After graduating from Seminary, I spent a lot of time reading different views about the Bible. I eventually reached the Zohar. This collection of midrash are considered the secret work of the Torah, according to Kabbalists. In addition, I read quite a bit about Messianic Judaism. Their view of the Bible differs greatly from the Seminary view.

I decided that the biblical interpretation that was being taught in Seminary was not the biblical interpretation the people heard when Jesus Christ (whose Hebraic name is Yeshua) preached. I went on a quest to learn what the people of Yeshua's day heard, and what they thought when the Scriptures were read. This quest led me to Dr. Anne Davis and The Bible Learning University. Dr. Davis was in search of the same thing I was searching for. She had made many discoveries that helped me in my quest. I earned the Ph.D. degree from The Bible Learning University in Hebraic Studies in Christianity concentrating on ancient Bible Studies methods.

Finally, I found someone who believed that the church has placed almost 1900 years of their theological ideas about the Scriptures, which differed from the original Hebraic thoughts, and in many places, possibly misinterpreted its original meaning. What is also important to hear is that the basic tenants of Yeshua as God's Messiah, my LORD and Savior are in the Bible. My faith in Yeshua is stronger now that I have learned from Dr. Davis how to study the Scriptures in the same manner that the people did in Yeshua's day.

I have included some articles that describe the differences between Greek learning methods and Hebraic learning methods. Please do not skip by them as irrelevant, unless you are familiar with the ancient Bible student method, because if you do, then the analysis and commentary that follows may become difficult to understand.

Our God is vast and infinite and so is His Word. May God bless you in your discovery of what God's Word is about.

In that vein of thought, we can consider the book of Jonah in light of Yeshua the Messiah. My study partner, Sandy, asked me if there is anything important to the name Jonah. As I considered this question I thought about the meaning of the word Jonah. This Hebrew word means "dove."   A dove is first encountered in the Noah story. When the rain had stopped and the water started to recede, Noah sent a dove out to look for dry land. When the dove returned with an olive branch, Noah knew that God had transformed the world. The world was restarted in peace and love.

When Yeshua was baptized in the Jordan River by John a dove came down from Heaven. The belief is that the dove is symbolic of the Holy Spirit. The love and grace of God descended upon the Earth in a "new form." Through the Holy Spirit the disciples of Yeshua brought God's love to a violent world. Yeshua preached that the Kingdom of God could be established on the Earth. A key component of the Kingdom of God is peace.

Can the Jonah story be viewed as a story about peace? Making peace with your enemies is not the major theme of the story, but it certainly can be a tributary of the main theme. Historically, it is known that the Assyrian Empire (Ninevites) was an enemy to many nations. The Northern Kingdom (Israel) and the Southern Kingdom (Judah) would have viewed Assyria as an enemy.

So, God sent a Hebrew prophet to Nineveh to bring a message to the people about repentance. Could another purpose of Jonah's mission to Nineveh be as a peacemaker? Why would a representative who viewed Nineveh as an enemy come to the city to warn it that the LORD was going to destroy them if they did not repent from their evil ways? The Middle Eastern nations and tribe who were conquered by the Assyrians would have been joyful if the LORD had destroyed the Empire before it destroyed them. Jonah's attempt to save Nineveh could be viewed as a message of peace. Could the Assyrians have viewed the Hebrews as a friend instead of an enemy?

You are probably thinking; the Assyrians destroyed the Northern Kingdom, so peace did not happen. However, the prophecy of the book of Jonah never happened. The Ninevites did not repent of their evil ways. Their Empire conquered the nations and tribes in the Middle East, and they did some of the worst things you can do to a fellow human.

Since the prophecy did not come true, neither did the peace that was hoped. If the people of Nineveh would have repented and changed their way, then the Hebrew people would have become their friends.

For us today, in the light of Yeshua, this story can tell us we should attempt to become friends with our enemies. Yeshua tells us to love our enemies in Matthew 5:44. The first step to loving an enemy is to make peace with them. Offering a gesture of some kind to soft the heart of the enemy may indeed work. Telling Nineveh about God's wrath and how to avoid it was the gesture of opening the door to peace. Loving our enemy might start by offering a gesture of peace. If we were all peacemakers, war would be eliminated from the world.

Jonah was the son of Amittai, who lived during the reign of Amaziah, king of Judah and Jeroboam II, king of Israel. The time frame was the first half of the eighth century B.C.E. (2 Kings 14:23-25). Jonah believed that the God of Israel and Judah was not the God of the Gentile nations who surrounded the Promised Land.

During Jonah's lifetime, the Assyrian Empire grew to the west and south of the River Euphrates. Israel and Judah could not escape from the power of the Assyrian Empire and eventually fell victim. It was through Jonah's prophecy that the Hebrews realized their God was also the God of the Gentiles. They also believed that God had empowered the Assyrians to punish them for their misdeeds and their pagan worship practices.

Jonah's vision from God was to take a message to the Assyrians about their deeds. Jonah resisted, probably because it was hard for him to accept that the God of the Hebrews would pardon a potential enemy. Jonah discovered the LORD existed everywhere because even though he tried to run away, the LORD found him.

Jonah submitted to the LORD and delivered the message. Jonah became angry when he saw the Gentiles accepted the LORD's message and repented while prophets were in Israel and Judah who offered the same message were being ignored.

The Main Difference between the Greek Method and Hebraic Method of Teaching

Once you are aware of the two teaching styles, you will be able to determine if you are in a class or reading a book, whether the analysis and/or teaching method is either in a Greek or Hebraic method. In the Greek method, it is automatically thought that the instructor is right because of advanced knowledge. In the college situation, it is because the professor has his/her Ph.D. in some areas of study, so one assumes that he or she knows everything about the topic. For example, Rodney Dangerfield played the role of a middle-aged man going to college. His English midterm was to write about Kurt Vonnegut Jr. Since he didn't understand any of Vonnegut's books, he hired Vonnegut himself to the write the midterm. When it was returned to him, the English Professor told Dangerfield that whoever wrote the paper knew nothing about Vonnegut. This is an example of the Greek method of teaching. Did the Ph.D. English professor think that she knew more about Vonnegut's writings than Vonnegut did?[2]

In the Greek teaching method, the professor or the instructor claims to be the authority. If you are attending a Bible study class and the class leader says "I will teach you the only way to understand this biblical book," consider the implications. This method is common since most seminaries and Bible colleges teach a Greek method of learning, which is the same method the church has been using for centuries.

Hebraic teaching methods are unique. The teacher wants the students to challenge what they hear. It is through questioning that a student can learn. In addition, the teacher wants his/her students to excel to a point where the student becomes the teacher.

It is said that if two rabbis come together to discuss a passage of Scripture, the result will be at least ten different opinions. All points of view are acceptable as long as biblical evidence can support the points. It is permissible and encourages students to have multiple opinions. There is a depth to God's Word, and God wants us to find all His messages that are placed in the Scriptures.

---

2 *Back to School*. Performed by Rodney Dangerfield. Hollywood: CA: Paper Clip Productions, 1986. DVD.

Seeking the meaning of the Scriptures beyond the literal meaning is essential to fully understanding God's Word.[3] The Greek method of learning the Scriptures has prevailed over the centuries. One problem is that only the literal interpretation of Scripture was often viewed as valid, as prompted by Martin Luther's "sola literalis" meaning that only the literal interpretation of Scripture was valid. The Fundamentalist movements of today are based on the literal interpretation of the Scripture. Therefore, they do not believe that God placed any deeper, hidden, or secret meanings in the Word.

The students of the Scriptures who learn through Hebraic training and understanding have drawn a different conclusion. The Hebrew language itself leads to different interpretations because of the construction of the language. The Hebraic method of Bible study opens avenues of thought about God's revelations in the Scripture that may have never been considered. A question may be raised about the Scripture being studied for which there may not be an immediate answer. If so, it becomes the responsibility of the learners to uncover the meaning. Also, remember that multiple opinions about the meaning of Scripture are also acceptable if Scripture can support them.

---

[3] Davis, Anne Kimball. *The Synoptic Gospels*. MP3. Albuquerque: NM: BibleInteract, 2012.

Methodology

The method employed is to use "Ancient Bible Study Methods" integrated with Jesus's day's customs and culture to examine the Hebrew and Christian Scriptures, thus gathering a more in-depth understanding by learning the Scriptures in the way the people of Jesus's day did.

I have titled the method of analyzing a passage of Scripture in a Hebraic manner the "Process of Discovery." The author developed this method, which combines various linguistic and cultural understanding areas. There are several sections to the process, and not all the parts apply to every passage of Scripture. The overall result of developing this process is to give the reader a framework for studying the Word in more depth.

The "Process of Discovery" starts with a Scripture passage. An examination of the linguistic structure of the passage is next. The linguistic structure includes parallelism, chiastic structures, and repetition. Formatting the passage in its linguistic form allows the reader to visualize what the first-century CE listener was hearing. Their corresponding sections label the chiasms, for example, A, B, C, B', A.' Not all passages of the Scriptures have a poetic form.

The next step is to "question the narrative." The narrative process of questioning the narrative assumes the reader knows nothing about the passage. Therefore, the questions go from simple to complex. The next task is to identify any linguistic patterns. Linguistic patterns include, but are not limited to, irony, simile, metaphor, symbolism, idioms, hyperbole, figurative language, personification, and allegory.

A review of any translation inconsistencies discovered between the English NAU version and Hebrew or Greek versions is done. Sometimes, a Hebrew or Greek word is translated in more than one way. Inconsistencies also can be created by the translation committee, which may have used traditional language instead of the actual translation. The decision of the translation committee is in the Preface or Introduction to the Bible. Perhaps some inconsistencies were intentionally added to convey some deeper meaning. An examination of every discrepancy is done.

The passage is analyzed for any echoes of the Hebrew Scriptures in the Christian Scriptures. An echo occurs using a passage from the Hebrew Scriptures in the Christian Scriptures.[4] Also, echoes are found when Torah (Genesis through Deuteronomy) passages are used in other Hebrew Bible books. Cross-references in the Scripture are references from one verse to another verse, which can help the reader understand the verse.

The names of persons mentioned in the passage are listed. Many Hebrew names have meaning and may be associated with places or actions. Jewish parents used to name their children based on what they felt God had in store for their children. An example is Abraham, whose original name was Abram and was changed to mean eternal father (God changed Abram's name to Abraham, showing a function he was to perform). When the Hebrew Bible gives names, many occurrences mean something unique. The same importance can occur for the names of places. The time to travel between locations can supply insight into the event.

Key phrases are identified in verses when they are essential to understanding that passage. There are no rules for selecting the keywords. Searching for other occurrences of the keywords in Scripture in concordance is necessary to understand the Word's usage; this must be done in either Hebrew or Greek, not in English. A classic Hebraic approach is to find the usage of a word in the Scripture by finding other verses that contain the Word. The usage of a word in its original language is discovered by searching the Scripture in the language of the Word. Verses that contain the Word are identified, and a pattern for the usage of the Word is discovered. Each verse is examined to see what the usage of the Word is, which may reveal a model for the Word's usage. The first usage of the Word in the Scripture, primarily if used in

---

[4] Mitzvot are the 613 commandments found in the Torah that please God. There are positive and negative commandments. The list was first development by Maimonides. The full list can be found at: ttp://www.jewfaq.org/613.htm.

the Torah, is essential for Hebrew words. The Christian Scriptures are used for Greek words to determine the Word usage in the Scripture. Sometimes, finding the equivalent Greek Word in the Septuagint can be beneficial as analyzing its Hebrew usage.

The Rules of Hillel are used when applicable. Hillel was a Torah scholar who lived shortly before Jesus' day. Hillel developed several rules for Torah students to interpret the Scriptures, which refer to halachic Midrash. In several cases, these rules are helpful in the analysis of the Scripture.

The cultural implications from the writing period are done after the linguistic analysis is completed. The culture is crucial because it is not explicitly referenced in the biblical narratives, as indicated earlier.

From the linguistic analysis and the cultural understanding, it is possible to get a deeper meaning of the Scripture beyond the plain text's literal meaning. That is what the listeners of Jesus' time were doing. They put linguistics and culture together without even having to contemplate it.

The analysis will lead to findings explaining the passage's meaning in Jesus' day. Most of the time, the Hebraic analysis leads to the desire for more in-depth analysis to fully understand what Jesus was discussing or what was happening to Him. Whatever the result, a new, more in-depth understanding of the Scripture is obtained.

The components of the Process of Discovery are:

Language

Process of Discovery

Linguistics Section

Linguistic Structure

Discussion

Questioning the Passage

Verse Comparison of citations or proof text

Translation Inconsistencies

Biblical Personalities

Biblical Locations

Phrase Study

New American Standard 1995	Hebrew	Septuagint
[1] The word of the LORD came to Jonah the son of Amittai saying, [2] "Arise, go to Nineveh the great city and cry against it, for their wickedness has come up before Me." [3] But Jonah rose up to flee to Tarshish from the presence of the LORD. So he went down to Joppa, found a ship which was going to Tarshish, paid the fare and went down into it to go with them to Tarshish from the presence of the LORD. [4] The LORD hurled a great wind on the sea and there was a great storm on the sea so that the ship was about to break up. [5] Then the sailors became	[1] וַיְהִי דְּבַר־יְהֹוָה אֶל־יוֹנָה בֶן־אֲמִתַּי לֵאמֹר: [2] קוּם לֵךְ אֶל־נִינְוֵה הָעִיר הַגְּדוֹלָה וּקְרָא עָלֶיהָ כִּי־עָלְתָה רָעָתָם לְפָנָי: [3] וַיָּקָם יוֹנָה לִבְרֹחַ תַּרְשִׁישָׁה מִלִּפְנֵי יְהֹוָה וַיֵּרֶד יָפוֹ וַיִּמְצָא אֳנִיָּה בָּאָה תַרְשִׁישׁ וַיִּתֵּן שְׂכָרָהּ וַיֵּרֶד בָּהּ לָבוֹא עִמָּהֶם תַּרְשִׁישָׁה מִלִּפְנֵי יְהֹוָה: [4] וַיהֹוָה הֵטִיל רוּחַ־גְּדוֹלָה אֶל־הַיָּם וַיְהִי סַעַר־גָּדוֹל בַּיָּם וְהָאֳנִיָּה חִשְּׁבָה לְהִשָּׁבֵר: [5] וַיִּירְאוּ הַמַּלָּחִים וַיִּזְעֲקוּ אִישׁ אֶל־אֱלֹהָיו וַיָּטִלוּ אֶת־הַכֵּלִים אֲשֶׁר בָּאֳנִיָּה אֶל־הַיָּם לְהָקֵל מֵעֲלֵיהֶם וְיוֹנָה יָרַד אֶל־יַרְכְּתֵי הַסְּפִינָה וַיִּשְׁכַּב וַיֵּרָדַם: [6] וַיִּקְרַב אֵלָיו רַב הַחֹבֵל	[1] Now the word of the LORD came to Jonas the son of Amathi, saying, [2] Rise, and go to Nineve, the great city, and preach in it; for the cry of its wickedness is come up to me. [3] But Jonas rose up to flee to Tharsis from the presence of the LORD. And he went down to Joppa, and found a ship going to Tharsis: and he paid his fare, and went up into it, to sail with them to Tharsis from the presence of the LORD. [4] And the LORD raised up a wind on the sea; and there was a great storm on the sea, and the ship was in danger of being broken. [5] And the sailors were alarmed, and cried every one to his god, and cast out the wares that were

New American Standard 1995	Hebrew	Septuagint
afraid and every man cried to his god, and they threw the cargo which was in the ship into the sea to lighten *it* for them. But Jonah had gone below into the hold of the ship, lain down and fallen sound asleep. 6 So the captain approached him and said, "How is it that you are sleeping? Get up, call on your god. Perhaps *your* god will be concerned about us so that we will not perish." 7 Each man said to his mate, "Come, let us cast lots so we may learn on whose account this calamity *has struck* us." So they cast lots and the lot fell on Jonah. 8 Then they said to him, "Tell us, now! On whose account *has* this calamity *struck* us? What is your occupation? And where do	וַיֹּ֣אמֶר ל֗וֹ מַה־לְּךָ֙ נִרְדָּ֔ם ק֚וּם קְרָ֣א אֶל־אֱלֹהֶ֔יךָ אוּלַ֞י יִתְעַשֵּׁ֧ת הָאֱלֹהִ֛ים לָ֖נוּ וְלֹ֥א נֹאבֵֽד׃ 7 וַיֹּאמְר֞וּ אִ֣ישׁ אֶל־רֵעֵ֗הוּ לְכוּ֙ וְנַפִּ֣ילָה גֽוֹרָל֔וֹת וְנֵ֣דְעָ֔ה בְּשֶׁלְּמִ֛י הָרָעָ֥ה הַזֹּ֖את לָ֑נוּ וַיַּפִּ֙לוּ֙ גּֽוֹרָל֔וֹת וַיִּפֹּ֥ל הַגּוֹרָ֖ל עַל־יוֹנָֽה׃ 8 וַיֹּאמְר֣וּ אֵלָ֔יו הַגִּידָה־נָּ֣א לָ֔נוּ בַּאֲשֶׁ֛ר לְמִי־הָרָעָ֥ה הַזֹּ֖את לָ֑נוּ מַה־מְּלַאכְתְּךָ֙ וּמֵאַ֣יִן תָּב֔וֹא מָ֣ה אַרְצֶ֔ךָ וְאֵֽי־מִזֶּ֥ה עַ֖ם אָֽתָּה׃ 9 וַיֹּ֥אמֶר אֲלֵיהֶ֖ם עִבְרִ֣י אָנֹ֑כִי וְאֶת־יְהוָ֞ה אֱלֹהֵ֤י הַשָּׁמַ֙יִם֙ אֲנִ֣י יָרֵ֔א אֲשֶׁר־עָשָׂ֥ה אֶת־הַיָּ֖ם וְאֶת־הַיַּבָּשָֽׁה׃ 10 וַיִּֽירְא֤וּ הָֽאֲנָשִׁים֙ יִרְאָ֣ה גְדוֹלָ֔ה וַיֹּאמְר֥וּ אֵלָ֖יו מַה־זֹּ֣את עָשִׂ֑יתָ כִּֽי־יָדְע֣וּ הָאֲנָשִׁ֗ים כִּֽי־מִלִּפְנֵ֤י יְהוָה֙ ה֣וּא בֹרֵ֔חַ כִּ֥י הִגִּ֖יד לָהֶֽם׃	in the ship into the sea, that it might be lightened of them. But Jonas was gone down into the hold of the ship, and was asleep, and snored. 6 And the shipmaster came to him, and said to him, Why snorest thou? arise, and call upon thy God, that God may save us, and we perish not. 7 And each man said to his neighbour, Come, let us cast lots, and find out for whose sake this mischief is upon us. So they cast lots, and the lot fell upon Jonas. 8 And they said to him, Tell us what is thine occupation, and whence comest thou, and of what country and what people art thou? 9 And he said to them, I am a servant of the LORD; and I worship the LORD God of heaven, who made the sea, and the dry *land*.

New American Standard 1995	Hebrew	Septuagint
you come from? What is your country? From what people are you?" ⁹ He said to them, "I am a Hebrew, and I fear the LORD God of heaven who made the sea and the dry land." ¹⁰ Then the men became extremely frightened and they said to him, "How could you do this?" For the men knew that he was fleeing from the presence of the LORD, because he had told them. ¹¹ So they said to him, "What should we do to you that the sea may become calm for us?"-- for the sea was becoming increasingly stormy. ¹² He said to them, "Pick me up and throw me into the sea. Then the sea will	¹¹וַיֹּאמְר֤וּ אֵלָיו֙ מַה־נַּ֣עֲשֶׂה לָּ֔ךְ וְיִשְׁתֹּ֥ק הַיָּ֖ם מֵֽעָלֵ֑ינוּ כִּ֥י הַיָּ֖ם הוֹלֵ֥ךְ וְסֹעֵֽר׃ ¹²וַיֹּ֣אמֶר אֲלֵיהֶ֗ם שָׂא֙וּנִי֙ וַהֲטִילֻ֣נִי אֶל־הַיָּ֔ם וְיִשְׁתֹּ֥ק הַיָּ֖ם מֵֽעֲלֵיכֶ֑ם כִּ֚י יוֹדֵ֣עַ אָ֔נִי כִּ֣י בְשֶׁלִּ֔י הַסַּ֧עַר הַגָּד֛וֹל הַזֶּ֖ה עֲלֵיכֶֽם׃ ¹³וַיַּחְתְּר֣וּ הָאֲנָשִׁ֗ים לְהָשִׁ֛יב אֶל־הַיַּבָּשָׁ֖ה וְלֹ֣א יָכֹ֑לוּ כִּ֣י הַיָּ֔ם הוֹלֵ֥ךְ וְסֹעֵ֖ר עֲלֵיהֶֽם׃ ¹⁴וַיִּקְרְא֨וּ אֶל־יְהוָ֜ה וַיֹּאמְר֗וּ אָנָּ֤ה יְהוָה֙ אַל־נָ֣א נֹאבְדָ֗ה בְּנֶ֙פֶשׁ֙ הָאִ֣ישׁ הַזֶּ֔ה וְאַל־תִּתֵּ֥ן עָלֵ֖ינוּ דָּ֣ם נָקִ֑יא כִּֽי־אַתָּ֣ה יְהוָ֔ה כַּאֲשֶׁ֥ר חָפַ֖צְתָּ עָשִֽׂיתָ׃ ¹⁵וַיִּשְׂאוּ֙ אֶת־יוֹנָ֔ה וַיְטִלֻ֖הוּ אֶל־הַיָּ֑ם וַיַּעֲמֹ֥ד הַיָּ֖ם מִזַּעְפּֽוֹ׃ ¹⁶וַיִּֽירְא֧וּ הָאֲנָשִׁ֛ים יִרְאָ֥ה	¹⁰ Then the men feared exceedingly, and said to him, What is this *that* thou hast done? for the men knew that he was fleeing from the face of the LORD, because he had told them. ¹¹ And they said to him, What shall we do to thee, that the sea may be calm to us? for the sea rose, and lifted its wave exceedingly. ¹² And Jonas said to them, Take me up, and cast me into the sea, and the sea shall be calm to you: for I know that for my sake this great tempest is upon you. ¹³ And the men tried hard to return to the land, and were not able: for the sea rose and grew more and more tempestuous against them. ¹⁴ And they cried to the LORD, and said, Forbid it, LORD: let us not perish for the sake of this man's life, and bring not righteous

New American Standard 1995	Hebrew	Septuagint
become calm for you, for I know that on account of me this great storm *has come* upon you." 13 However, the men rowed *desperately* to return to land but they could not, for the sea was becoming *even* stormier against them. 14 Then they called on the LORD and said, "We earnestly pray, O LORD, do not let us perish on account of this man's life and do not put innocent blood on us; for You, O LORD, have done as You have pleased." 15 So they picked up Jonah, threw him into the sea, and the sea stopped its raging. 16 Then the men feared the LORD greatly, and they offered a sacrifice to the LORD and made vows.	גְדוֹלָה אֶת־יְהוָה וַיִּזְבְּחוּ־ זֶבַח לַיהוָֹה וַיִּדְּרוּ נְדָרִים:	blood upon us: for thou, LORD, hast done as thou wouldest. 15 So they took Jonas, and cast him out into the sea: and the sea ceased from its raging. 16 And the men feared the LORD very greatly, and offered a sacrifice to the LORD, and vowed vows.

New American Standard 1995	Hebrew	Septuagint
[17] And the LORD appointed a great fish to swallow Jonah, and Jonah was in the stomach of the fish three days and three nights.		

Process of Discovery

Linguistics Section

Linguistic Structure

[Commandment from the LORD][1] The word of the LORD came to Jonah the son of Amittai saying, [2] "Arise, go to Nineveh the great city and cry against it, for their wickedness has come up before Me."

[Rejection of the command] [3] But Jonah rose up to flee to Tarshish from the presence of the LORD. So he went down to Joppa, found a ship which was going to Tarshish, paid the fare and went down into it to go with them to Tarshish from the presence of the LORD.

A [4] The LORD hurled a great wind on the sea and **there was a great storm on the sea** so that the ship was about to break up. [5] Then the sailors became afraid and every man cried to his god, and they threw the cargo which was in the ship into the sea to lighten *it* for them. But Jonah had gone below into the hold of the ship, lain down and fallen sound asleep.

B [6] So the captain approached him and said, "How is it that you are sleeping? Get up, call on your god. Perhaps *your* god will be concerned about us so that we will not perish." [7] Each man said to his mate, "Come, let us cast lots so we may learn on whose account this calamity *has struck* us." So they cast lots and the lot fell on Jonah. [8] Then they said to him, "Tell us, now! **On whose account *has* this calamity *struck* us?** What is your occupation? And where do you come from? What is your country? From what people are you?"

C [Jonah's words] [9] He said to them, "I am a Hebrew, and I fear the LORD God of heaven who made the sea and the dry land."

D [People's words][10] Then the men became extremely frightened and they said to him, "How could you do this?"

E For the men knew that he was fleeing from the presence of the LORD, because he had told them.

D' [People's words] [11] So they said to him, "What should we do to you that the sea may become calm for us?"-- for the sea was becoming increasingly stormy.

C' [Jonah's words] [12] He said to them, "Pick me up and throw me into the sea. Then the sea will become calm for you, for I know that on account of me this great storm *has come* upon you."

B' [13] However, the men rowed *desperately* to return to land but they could not, for the seas becoming *even* stormier against them. [14] Then they called on the LORD and said, "We earnestly pray, O LORD, **do not let us perish on account of this man's life and do not put innocent blood on us**; for You, O LORD, have done as You have pleased."

A' [15] So they picked up Jonah, threw him into the sea, and the **sea stopped its raging**. [16] Then the men feared the LORD greatly, and they offered a sacrifice to the LORD and made vows.

[God's response to Jonah's running away] [17] And the LORD appointed a great fish to swallow Jonah, and Jonah was in the stomach of the fish three days and three nights.

Discussion

The book of Jonah commences like other books of the prophets, saying that the word of the LORD came to Jonah. The first two verses were commands from the LORD. The third verse is Jonah's response to the LORD. The rest of the chapter is a chiasm which tells us that Jonah was fleeing from the LORD. The last verse is an action of the LORD in response to Jonah's running away.

Questioning the Passage

(

1. Who was Jonah? (v. 1)

    Jonah the prophet is mentioned in 2 Kings. He lived and prophesied during the reign of King Jeroboam[5] son of Joash. "The Sages identify Jonah as the prophet sent by Elijah to anoint Yehu[6] as King of the Ten tribes (2 Kings 9:1). Pirkei DeRabbi Eliezer[7] identifies Jonah as a child whom Elijah revived (1 Kings 17). According to a tradition cited by Abarbanel[8], Jonah lived more than 120 years.

2. Is anything known of Jonah's father Amittai? (v. 2)

    "Father of the prophet Jonah (II Kings, xiv. 25; Jonah, i. 1). According to rabbinical sources (Yer. Suk. v. 55*a*; Gen. R. xcviii.; Yalḳ., Jonah, § 550) Amittai came from the tribe of Zebulon and lived at Zarephath. There is a tradition that the widow who sustained the prophet Elijah there (I Kings, xvii. 9-24) was Amittai's wife, and that the child whom Elijah revived was Jonah (Pirḳe R. El. xxxiii.)."[9]

3. What is the significance of the city of Nineveh? (v. 2)

    The city of Nineveh was the capital of the Assyrian Empire.

---

[5] When Rehoboam convened Israel at Shechem, after his father's death, to confirm his own succession to the throne, Jeroboam, apprised of what had occurred, returned. He seems to have been the spokesman for assembled Israel and to have represented their demands for relief from the "grievous yoke." Upon the refusal of Rehoboam to accede to their demands, and the failure of the attempt to coerce the complainants into submission, which led to the stoning of Adoram, the ten northern tribes asserted their independence by proclaiming Jeroboam their king, the prophet Shemaiah preventing any warlike measures on the part of Rehoboam (I Kings xii. 1-24; II Chron. x., xi. 1-4). Source: JEROBOAM - JewishEncyclopedia.com. Accessed December 22, 2016.

[6] Son of Jehoshaphat and grandson of Nimshi, founder of the fifth Israelitish dynasty (842-743 B.C.); died 815 B.C., in the twenty-eighth year of his reign. Source: Jehu - JewishEncyclopedia.com. Accessed December 22, 2016.

[7] Haggadic midrashic work on Genesis, part of Exodus, and a few sentences of Numbers; ascribed to R. Eliezer b. Hyrcanus, and composed in Italy shortly after 833. Source: JewishEncyclopedia.com. Accessed December 22, 2016.

[8] **A**brabanel (Abravanel). Isaac ben Judah (1437–1508), Jewish statesman, commentator, and philosopher.. Source: Bowker, John. "Isaac Abravanel." In *The Concise Oxford Dictionary of World Religions*. Oxford: Oxford University Press, 2005.

[9] JewishEncyclopedia.com. Accessed December 22, 2016.

4. Why do the Scriptures say that the city of Nineveh was a great city? (v. 2)

During the height of the Empire the city is believed to have had a population that exceeded 120,000 people making it a very large city for its time.

5. Why had the wickedness of the city of Nineveh risen to the LORD? (v. 2)

There are several reasons why the LORD was concerned about the wickedness of the city of Nineveh. According to Ibn Ezra[10], one reason offered was that the people of the city of Nineveh did not worship idols. Rather their wickedness was limited to moral and social sins. Therefore, God had compassion on them and gave the people an opportunity to repent.

According to Radak[11], another possibility is that the sin of Nineveh was in the area of robbery and oppression, thus paralleling the evils of the generation of the flood and the Sodomites. This form of behavior was extremely destructive to the social order and therefore, since God wanted to preserve his creation, he decided to intervene.

According to Malbim[12], another reason is that God intended to raise Assyria to punish the Northern Kingdom of Israel because of the Northern Kingdom's sins. Therefore, God sent Jonah to Nineveh so that the people of Nineveh could repent and become worthy of their future mission.

6. Why did Jonah decide to flee to Tarshish? (v. 3)

Jonah fled to Tarshish so that he would not have to bring God's message to the Ninevites. For if the Ninevites had repented and God would have forgiven them, Jonah could have rationalized that he would be condemning Israel, who constantly ignored the prophetic call

---

[10] Scholar and writer; born 1089-1167; died Jan. 28. Source: JewishEncyclopedia.com. Accessed December 22, 2016.

[11] Rabbi at Corfu, and later at Patros, Greece, at the beginning of the sixteenth century. Source: JewishEncyclopedia.com. Accessed April 3, 3017

[12] Russian rabbi, preacher, and Hebraist; born at Volochisk, Volhynia, in 1809; died at Kiev Sept. 18, 1879. The name "Malbim" is derived from the initials of his name (מלבים). Source: JewishEncyclopedia.com. Accessed December 22, 2016.

for repentance.

According to the Sages, Jonah probably had two concerns: (1) if the Ninevites would have repented and God would have spared them, he might have poured his wrath out against Israel for not having similarly repented in the face of repeated divine expectations; and (2) the survivors of the Assyrian attack could have accused him of prophesying falsely, resulting in Jonah's profaning the name of God.

Perhaps, Jonah the prophet may have been fundamentally opposed to forgiveness after repentance. It is written in the Talmud, what is the sinner's punishment? If the LORD forgave the Ninevites for their sin, then what would have been their punishment?[13]

7. What is the significance of the city of Tarshish? (v. 3)

The city of Tarshish was in the south of Spain, therefore it was a long way from Israel. In those days people believed that the LORD could not reach them once they left the land of Israel because they believed the LORD only resided in the land of Israel while on earth.

If Jonah believed that the LORD could not reach him why would he think that the LORD could reach Nineveh? A possible answer is that Jonah could have thought that the LORD could not reach him when he was outside of Israel but that the LORD could reach the Gentiles in Nineveh.

8. Why is the city of Tarshish repeated three times in verse three? (v. 3)

Repetition is used in the Hebrew Scriptures to emphasize a point. The point being that Jonah was running away from the LORD as fast as he could and as far away from the LORD as he could.

9. Why does verse four say that the LORD hurled a great wind and then a great storm? Does a great storm imply a great wind, if so, why the repetition?

---

[13] Scherman, Nosson, Meir Zlotowitz, Sheah Brander, and Menachem Davis. "Jonah." In The Prophets: The Later Prophets with a Commentary Anthologized from the Rabbinic Writings. Brooklyn, NY: Mesorah Publications, 2013. p. 225.

The Scripture says that the LORD hurled a great wind and then a great storm tells us that natural occurrences did not bring the storm about but rather that it was God who brought the storm. That would account for the repetition.[14]

10. Why did the men decide to lighten the ship by throwing the cargo overboard? (v. 5)

Pirkei DeRabbi Eliezer 10:31 records that because of the ineffectiveness of the sailors' prayers to their own gods they decided to throw their idols into the sea thus lightening the boat but more importantly showing the LORD that they did not believe in their idols anymore and believed in Jonah's God.[15]

11. How could Jonah sleep through this great wind and great storm? (v. 5)

An interpretation of this verse is that Jonah could not sleep, so he went into the hold of the ship where the sailors were praying to their gods because Jonah did not feel that he should call upon the LORD since he was running away from the LORD. When Jonah went into the hold of the ship he expected to die.

12. Why did the captain of the ship ask Jonah to call upon his God to save them? (v. 6)

Since it was clear to the sailors that calling upon their gods was not going to help their situation, they must have figured that it would not hurt to ask Jonah to call upon his God.

13. Why did the crew decide that one of the crew or passengers was causing the storm? (v. 7)

The crew needed to explain why this great storm was upon them. Since it was a divine storm, it must have been greater than any storm they had ever experienced. In ancient days omens like these were interpreted as divine intervention. Therefore, either one of the crew or one of the passengers was the cause of the storm.

14. Why did they ask him what country he was from? (v. 8)

---

[14] IBID. p. 227.

[15] IBID.

The sailors asked this question of Jonah to determine whether he was the cause of their problems.

15. Why did the men get frightened when they learned that Jonah was running away from the presence of the LORD? (v. 10)

The men on the boat must have known something about the God of Israel. Since they determined that Jonah was causing the storm and with their knowledge of the God of Israel, they became frightened because they probably knew that the LORD was after Jonah and that they could die because of Jonah's fleeing from the LORD.

16. Why did the men not immediately throw Jonah overboard rather they tried to row desperately to return the land? (v. 13)

Perhaps they were trying not to sacrifice Jonah's life to satisfy the LORD. If they could have rowed to land and safety, they could have escaped the wrath of the LORD's storm and Jonah's life would have been spared.

Another idea is that the men wanted Jonah off their ship without killing him, so they would not feel guilty.

17. When the sailors decided to call upon the LORD does that mean that they believed in the LORD? (v. 14)

Since they offered their prayers to their idols without any effect, they decided to offer their prayers to the LORD. This does not indicate that they believed in the LORD and thus abandoned their idols, but rather it means that they included the LORD in their collection of gods.

Main/Center Point

What Jonah learned from this experience was that you cannot flee from God. For the people of Israel this prophecy would have told them that the LORD God reigns all over the earth not just in Israel and in Judah. The idea of monotheism was starting to take a firm shape. In order to have true monotheism the belief that other nations have different gods then you has to be overcome. By the sailors throwing their idols overboard because their prayers to their idols did nothing, it is like saying that they believed in the one true God, which is the God of Israel.

Symbols

1. What is the symbolism of Jonah being swallowed by the great fish and being in its stomach for three days and three nights? (v. 17)

It should be noted that in the Tanakh and the Septuagint that verse seventeen is actually a part of chapter two and is verse one of the chapter. The LORD chose a big fish to be God's agent and to act for God upon the earth by swallowing Jonah. God chose a fish that would be large enough to hold Jonah in his stomach. The LORD does not like to upset the natural order but rather work within the framework of nature which he set up.[16]

Three is a number used in the Scripture to denote divine intervention. Therefore, God did not intervene until the third day.

People's names

1. אֲמִתַּי *Amittay* **Meaning:** 'true,' the father of Jonah

2. יוֹנָה *Yonah* **Meaning:** an Israeli prophet

Name of places

1. תַּרְשִׁישׁ *Tarshish* **Meaning:** a son of Javan, the name his descendants, and the name of their land, also a port on the Mediterranean, and a city in Spain.

2. יָפוֹ *Yapho* or יָפוֹא *Yapho* **Meaning:** a seaport city of Israel

---

[16] IBID. p. 229.

Word Study

1. קָרָא *qara* **Meaning:** *to call, proclaim, read* (v. 2)

   [NAU] **Genesis 1:5** God **called** the light day, and the darkness He called night. And there was evening and there was morning, one day. (Gen. 1:5 NAU)

   [NAU] **Genesis 1:8** God **called** the expanse heaven. And there was evening and there was morning, a second day. (Gen. 1:8 NAU)

   [NAU] **Isaiah 22:12** Therefore in that day the LORD GOD of hosts **called** *you* to weeping, to wailing, To shaving the head and to wearing sackcloth (Isa. 22:12 NAU)

From the Theological Wordbook of the Old Testament: "The verb may represent the specification of a name. Naming is sometimes an assertion of sovereignty over the thing named. God's creating entailed naming and numbering the stars (Psa 147:4), the darkness (Gen 1:5), indeed all things (Isa 40:26). God presented the animals to Adam to assert his relative sovereignty over them (Gen 2:19). God sovereignly called Cyrus by name (note that election to a task is involved here, Isa 45:4).

Conclusion: Based on the meaning and usage of the word, the meaning "to call" is the better translation. Jonah was told by the LORD to go to Nineveh and to call out their sins. Jonah was to name the sins of the people. Probably the people did not know that what they were doing was sinful to the LORD. Jonah called out their sins and identified them for them.

Scripture cross references

Verse 1 2Ki 14:25; Mat 12:39-41; Mat 16:4; Luk 11:29, Luk 11:30, 32

Verse 3 Isa 23:1, Isa 23:6, 10; Jer 10:9; Gen 4:16; Psa 139:7, Psa 139:9, 10; Jos 19:46; 2Ch 2:16; Ezr 3:7; Act 9:36, Act 9:43

Verse 4 Psa 107:23-28; Psa 135:6, Psa 135:7

Verse 5 1Ki 18:26; Act 27:18, Act 27:19, 38

Verse 6 Psa 107:28; 2Sa 12:22; Amo 5:15

Verse 7 Jos 7:14-18; 1Sa 10:20, 1Sa 10:21; 1Sa 14:41, 1Sa 14:42; Act 1:23-26; Num 32:23; Pro 16:33

Verse 8 Jos 7:19; 1Sa 14:43; Gen 47:3; 1Sa 30:13

Verse 12 2Sa 24:17; 1Ch 21:17

Verse 17 Mat 12:40; Mat 16:4

Culture Section

Discussion

"The word of the LORD came to me" was one of the various ways used by the prophets to tell us that the LORD gave the prophet a vision. There are several other ways that prophets let us know that they had a vision. "The word of the LORD came to me" means "I was in a trance state or asleep and saw visions, I prophesied, I transcended the material world and was communing with God who is Spirit."[17]

Questioning the passage

1. Did Jonah believe that he could escape from the presence of the LORD

   There was the belief of a localized presence of the LORD which was in Israel and Judah. Even though the Hebrews believed in the one and only true God they did believe that the essence of the LORD resided in the Promised Land. Therefore, Jonah must have believed even though the LORD is God and the essence of the LORD was in the Promised Land, that running away from the Promised Land might allow him to escape the LORD's directive.

---

[17] Errico, Rocco A., and George M. Lamsa. *Aramaic Light on Ezekiel, Daniel, and the Minor Prophets: A Commentary Based on the Aramaic Language and Ancient Near Eastern Customs.* p. 159.

2. How are lots cast in Jonah's day? (v. 7)

"Means of determining chances. Primitive peoples, and occasionally those on a higher plane of culture, resort to lots for the purposes of augury. They spin a coconut or entangle strips of leather in order to obtain an omen. Thieves especially are detected by the casting of lots, etc. (Tylor, "Primitive Culture," German ed., i. 78-82). The pagans on a ship with Jonah under stress of a storm cast lots in order to find out who among them had incurred the Divine anger (Jonah i. 7). Haman resorted to the lot when he intended to destroy the Jews (Esth. iii. 7). The Greek heroes cast their lots into Agamemnon's helmet in order to ascertain who should fight with Hector ("Iliad," vii. 171). In ancient Italy oracles with carved lots were used. "[18]

Thoughts

Through this part of the Jonah story we learn that the LORD is everywhere on Earth. For us today, we already know that. For the people in Jonah's time, they did not know this. Jonah learns that one cannot escape the LORD. The command Jonah was given upset him so much that he fled from the Promised Land. The LORD followed Jonah by placing His breath (ruach) upon the waters and brought a great storm. In order to save the crew and passengers, Jonah decided to have himself thrown overboard. It was a generous offer that he made. The last verse in the English versions concerns the large fish that the LORD brought up to swallow Jonah. In the Hebrew versions this last verse is the first verse of the next chapter.

---

[18] LOTS - JewishEncyclopedia.com. Accessed December 22, 2016.

New American Standard 1995	Hebrew	Septuagint
[1] Then Jonah prayed to the LORD his God from the stomach of the fish, [2] and he said, "I called out of my distress to the LORD, And He answered me. I cried for help from the depth of Sheol; You heard my voice. [3] "For You had cast me into the deep, Into the heart of the seas, And the current engulfed me. All Your breakers and billows passed over me. [4] "So I said, 'I have been expelled from Your sight. Nevertheless I will look again toward Your holy temple.' [5] "Water encompassed me to the point of death. The	[1] וַיְמַ֤ן יְהוָה֙ דָּ֣ג גָּד֔וֹל לִבְלֹ֖עַ אֶת־יוֹנָ֑ה וַיְהִ֤י יוֹנָה֙ בִּמְעֵ֣י הַדָּ֔ג שְׁלֹשָׁ֥ה יָמִ֖ים וּשְׁלֹשָׁ֥ה לֵילֽוֹת׃ [2] וַיִּתְפַּלֵּ֣ל יוֹנָ֔ה אֶל־יְהוָ֖ה אֱלֹהָ֑יו מִמְּעֵ֖י הַדָּגָֽה׃ [3] וַיֹּ֗אמֶר קָ֠רָאתִי מִצָּ֥רָה לִ֛י אֶל־יְהוָ֖ה וַֽיַּעֲנֵ֑נִי מִבֶּ֧טֶן שְׁא֛וֹל שִׁוַּ֖עְתִּי שָׁמַ֥עְתָּ קוֹלִֽי׃ [4] וַתַּשְׁלִיכֵ֤נִי מְצוּלָה֙ בִּלְבַ֣ב יַמִּ֔ים וְנָהָ֖ר יְסֹבְבֵ֑נִי כָּל־מִשְׁבָּרֶ֥יךָ וְגַלֶּ֖יךָ עָלַ֥י עָבָֽרוּ׃ [5] וַאֲנִ֣י אָמַ֔רְתִּי נִגְרַ֖שְׁתִּי מִנֶּ֣גֶד עֵינֶ֑יךָ אַ֚ךְ אוֹסִ֣יף לְהַבִּ֔יט אֶל־הֵיכַ֖ל קָדְשֶֽׁךָ׃ [6] אֲפָפ֤וּנִי מַ֙יִם֙ עַד־נֶ֔פֶשׁ תְּה֖וֹם יְסֹבְבֵ֑נִי ס֖וּף חָב֥וּשׁ לְרֹאשִֽׁי׃ [7] לְקִצְבֵ֤י הָרִים֙ יָרַ֔דְתִּי הָאָ֛רֶץ בְּרִחֶ֥יהָ בַעֲדִ֖י לְעוֹלָ֑ם וַתַּ֧עַל מִשַּׁ֛חַת חַיַּ֖י יְהוָ֥ה אֱלֹהָֽי׃ [8] בְּהִתְעַטֵּ֤ף עָלַי֙ נַפְשִׁ֔י אֶת־יְהוָ֖ה זָכָ֑רְתִּי וַתָּב֤וֹא אֵלֶ֙יךָ֙ תְּפִלָּתִ֔י אֶל־הֵיכַ֖ל	[1] Now the Lord had commanded a great whale to swallow up Jonas: and Jonas was in the belly of the whale three days and three nights. [2] And Jonas prayed to the Lord his God out of the belly of the whale, [3] and said, I cried in my affliction to the Lord my God, and he hearkened to me, *even* to my cry out of the belly of hell: thou heardest my voice. [4] Thou didst cast me into the depths of the heart of the sea, and the floods compassed me: all thy billows and thy waves have passed upon me. [5] And I said, I am cast out

New American Standard 1995	Hebrew	Septuagint
great deep engulfed me, Weeds were wrapped around my head. 6 "I descended to the roots of the mountains. The earth with its bars *was* around me forever, But You have brought up my life from the pit, O LORD my God. 7 "While I was fainting away, I remembered the LORD, And my prayer came to You, Into Your holy temple. 8 "Those who regard vain idols Forsake their faithfulness, 9 But I will sacrifice to You With the voice of thanksgiving. That which I have vowed I will pay. Salvation is from the LORD."	קָדְשֶֽׁךָ׃ 9 מְשַׁמְּרִים הַבְלֵי־שָׁוְא חַסְדָּם יַעֲזֹֽבוּ׃ 10 וַאֲנִי בְּקוֹל תּוֹדָה אֶזְבְּחָה־לָּךְ אֲשֶׁר נָדַרְתִּי אֲשַׁלֵּמָה יְשׁוּעָתָה לַיהוָֽה׃ ס 11 וַיֹּאמֶר יְהוָה לַדָּג וַיָּקֵא אֶת־יוֹנָה אֶל־הַיַּבָּשָֽׁה׃ פ	of thy presence: shall I indeed look again toward thy holy temple? 6 Water was poured around me to the soul: the lowest deep compassed me, my head went down 7 to the clefts of the mountains; I went down into the earth, whose bars are the everlasting barriers: yet, O Lord my God, let my ruined life be restored. 8 When my soul was failing me, I remembered the Lord; and may my prayer come to thee into thy holy temple. 9 They that observe vanities and lies have forsaken their own mercy. 10 But I will sacrifice to thee with the voice of

New American Standard 1995	Hebrew	Septuagint
10 Then the LORD commanded the fish, and it vomited Jonah up onto the dry land.		praise and thanksgiving: all that I have vowed I will pay to thee, the Lord of *my* salvation. the Lord commanded 11 And the whale, and it cast up Jonas on the dry *land*.

Process of Discovery

Linguistics Section

Linguistic Structure

A [1:17] And the LORD appointed **a great fish to swallow Jonah**, and Jonah was in the stomach of the fish three days and three nights.

> **B** [1] Then Jonah prayed to the LORD his God from the stomach of the fish, [2] and he said, "I called out of my distress to the LORD, And He answered me. **I cried for help from the depth of Sheol**; You heard my voice.

> > C [3] "For You had cast me into the deep, Into the heart of the seas, And the current engulfed me. All Your breakers and billows passed over me. [4] "So I said, 'I have been expelled from Your sight. Nevertheless I will look again toward Your holy temple.' [5] "Water encompassed me to the point of death. The great deep engulfed me, Weeds were wrapped around my head.

> **B'** [6] "I descended to the roots of the mountains. The earth with its bars *was* around me forever, **But You have brought up my life from the pit**, O LORD my God. [7] "While I was fainting away, I remembered the LORD, And my prayer came to You, Into Your holy temple. [8] "Those who regard vain idols Forsake their faithfulness, [9] But I will sacrifice to You With the voice of thanksgiving. That which I have vowed I will pay. Salvation is from the LORD."

A' [10] Then the LORD commanded the **fish, and it vomited Jonah up** onto the dry land.

Discussion

In the New American Standard 1995 version of the Bible the verse about Jonah being swallowed by the big fish is in chapter one. In several other versions of the Scriptures this verse is a part of chapter two. For the completeness of the chiasm in chapter two it is necessary to include verse 1:17 in this chapter. The chiasm commences with Jonah being swallowed by the Great Fish and it ends with the Great Fish spitting out Jonah.

Questioning the Passage

1. How could Jonah have survived in the belly of a fish for three days? (v. 1:17)

   The large fish which swallowed Jonah was acting as an agent of the LORD. Normally Jonah could not have survived the belly of the fish for three days. However, he was able to survive because God wanted him to survive. If Jonah was in the belly of the fish he would have lasted about one hour, if that much, because he would have run out of oxygen. Jonah surviving for three days symbolically tells us that he drowned and died and was reborn three days later. It can be said that Jonah died to his old self, the self that ran away from the commandments of the LORD and was reborn as a faithful disciple of the LORD. He experienced a transformation.

2. Why is the belly of the fish called Sheol in verse 2?

   The belly of the fish is called Sheol to correspond with the symbolism that Jonah died and was reborn. This also could tell us that those who do not obey the commands of the LORD will be going to Sheol. Having been swallowed by the big fish Jonah probably figured that he was going to die.

3. What are the LORD's breakers and billows? (v. 3)

   The Hebrew for "breakers and billows" can both be translated as waves. Therefore, there is a repetition within the verse telling us that Jonah was actually sinking because the waves of the sea were covering him, and because it is repeated with a synonym it gives it a stronger emphasis.

4. What does it mean to look toward the Holy Temple? (v. 4)

   To look toward the holy temple, in Jonah's day, meant to offer prayers to the LORD.

5. What is the symbolism of having weeds wrapped around Jonah's head? (v. 5)

There is no symbolism about the weeds wrapped around Jonah's head. This is just another emphasis that Jonah was thrown into the sea.

6. What are the bars of the earth? (v. 6)

No information on this expression has yet been found. The Midrash would have to be explored.

7. What is the meaning of verses 8 & 9?

These two verses refer to people who were idol worshipers. It is also possible that these verses refer to the sailors who did not believe in the LORD. It is a part of the prayer Jonah offered to the LORD which reminded him that he must place his trust in the LORD and not in other idols or false gods. Jonah acknowledges that salvation only comes from the LORD.

Main/Center Point

Jonah came to understand that salvation comes only from the LORD. He also learned that he could not run away from the LORD and that he needed to obey the LORD's commandments that were laid out before him. We are also told that even if we openly disobey the LORD that the LORD is willing to take us back as long as we are willing to admit to our mistake and ask for forgiveness.

Symbols

1. What is the symbolism of the number three?

The main symbolism of the number three is that it represents the LORD. It is emphasized in Christianity because of Trinity doctrine.

2. What are the roots of the mountains? (v. 6)

The roots of the mountains can also be translated as the base of the mountains, or the clefts of the mountain. The roots of the mountain could be symbolic of Jonah not wanting to heed the commands of the LORD. The Temple existed on the top of Mount Sinai. Since ancient people believed that the closer you could get to the firmament, the closer you could get to God, going to the roots of the mountain would get you as far away from God as possible.

Translation Inconsistencies

The following is not a translation inconsistency but is interesting, nevertheless. The Hebrew says that a male fish swallowed Jonah. However, when Jonah prayed to the LORD from inside the belly of the fish, the Hebrew says that it was a female fish. There is not a lot of data about why a male fish swallows Jonah and becomes a pregnant female fish. When the book of Jonah was written people probably got a good chuckle out of it.

Jonah 2:1 ^{WTT} וַיְמַ֤ן יְהוָה֙ דָּ֣ג גָּד֔וֹל לִבְלֹ֖עַ אֶת־יוֹנָ֑ה וַיְהִ֤י יוֹנָה֙ בִּמְעֵ֣י הַדָּ֔ג שְׁלֹשָׁ֥ה יָמִ֖ים וּשְׁלֹשָׁ֥ה לֵילֽוֹת׃

Jonah 2:2 ^{WTT} וַיִּתְפַּלֵּ֣ל יוֹנָ֔ה אֶל־יְהוָ֖ה אֱלֹהָ֑יו מִמְּעֵ֖י הַדָּגָֽה׃

Jonah 2:10 וַיֹּ֥אמֶר יְהוָ֖ה לַדָּ֑ג וַיָּקֵ֥א אֶת־יוֹנָ֖ה אֶל־הַיַּבָּשָֽׁה׃

People's names

1. יוֹנָה *Yonah* **Meaning:** an Israeli prophet

Scripture cross references

Verse 2 1Sa 30:6; Psa 18:4-6; Psa 22:24; Psa 120:1; Psa 18:5, Psa 18:6; Psa 86:13; Psa 88:1-7

Verse 3 Psa 18:5; Psa 116:3; Isa 38:10; Mat 16:18; Job 33:28; Psa 16:10; Psa 30:3; Isa 38:17

Verse 9 Psa 50:14, Psa 50:23; Jer 33:11; Hos 14:2; Job 22:27; Ecc 5:4, Ecc 5:5; Psa 3:8; Isa 45:1

Culture Section

Discussion

Jonah makes a vow while in the belly of the fish. Semitic tradition was that if you made a vow, especially to the LORD, then you carried it out no matter how long it took and no matter how many resources it took.

Thoughts

Jonah decided to run from the LORD because he did not want to do what the LORD had commanded. In this chapter we learn of God's forgiveness and salvation. Jonah offered his prayers to the LORD, admitting to his mistake in telling the LORD that he would obey him faithfully. Because of this admission of guilt and repentance the LORD saved Jonah by having a large fish spit him out on land. Somewhere in most people's lives they reject what the LORD God has to offer them. However, God will not allow people to just go into the abyss but rather God will allow us to return into a relationship of discipleship with him. Therefore, we see in this chapter the love God has for each and every one of us..

New American Standard 1995	Hebrew	Septuagint
[1] Now the word of the LORD came to Jonah the second time, saying,	וַיְהִ֧י דְבַר־יְהוָ֛ה אֶל־יוֹנָ֖ה שֵׁנִ֥ית לֵאמֹֽר׃ [1]	[1] And the word of the Lord came to Jonas the second time, saying,
[2] "Arise, go to Nineveh the great city and proclaim to it the proclamation which I am going to tell you."	[2] ק֛וּם לֵ֥ךְ אֶל־נִֽינְוֵ֖ה הָעִ֣יר הַגְּדוֹלָ֑ה וִּקְרָ֤א אֵלֶ֙יהָ֙ אֶת־הַקְּרִיאָ֔ה אֲשֶׁ֥ר אָנֹכִ֖י דֹּבֵ֥ר אֵלֶֽיךָ׃	[2] Rise, go to Nineve, the great city, and preach in it according to the former preaching which I spoke to thee of.
[3] So Jonah arose and went to Nineveh according to the word of the LORD. Now Nineveh was an exceedingly great city, a three days' walk.	[3] וַיָּ֣קָם יוֹנָ֗ה וַיֵּ֛לֶךְ אֶל־נִֽינְוֵ֖ה כִּדְבַ֣ר יְהוָ֑ה וְנִֽינְוֵ֗ה הָיְתָ֤ה עִיר־גְּדוֹלָה֙ לֵֽאלֹהִ֔ים מַהֲלַ֖ךְ שְׁלֹ֥שֶׁת יָמִֽים׃	[3] And Jonas arose, and went to Nineve, as the Lord had spoken. Now Nineve was an exceeding great city, of about three days' journey.
[4] Then Jonah began to go through the city one day's walk; and he cried out and said, "Yet forty days and Nineveh will be overthrown."	[4] וַיָּ֤חֶל יוֹנָה֙ לָב֣וֹא בָעִ֔יר מַהֲלַ֖ךְ י֣וֹם אֶחָ֑ד וַיִּקְרָא֙ וַיֹּאמַ֔ר ע֚וֹד אַרְבָּעִ֣ים י֔וֹם וְנִֽינְוֵ֖ה נֶהְפָּֽכֶת׃	[4] And Jonas began to enter into the city about a day's journey, and he proclaimed, and said, Yet three days, and Nineve shall be overthrown.
[5] Then the people of Nineveh believed in God; and they called a fast and put on sackcloth from the	[5] וַֽיַּאֲמִ֛ינוּ אַנְשֵׁ֥י נִֽינְוֵ֖ה בֵּֽאלֹהִ֑ים וַיִּקְרְאוּ־צוֹם֙ וַיִּלְבְּשׁ֣וּ שַׂקִּ֔ים מִגְּדוֹלָ֖ם וְעַד־קְטַנָּֽם׃	[5] And the men of Nineve believed God, and proclaimed a fast, and put on sackcloths, from the greatest
	[6] וַיִּגַּ֤ע הַדָּבָר֙ אֶל־מֶ֣לֶךְ נִֽינְוֵ֔ה וַיָּ֙קָם֙ מִכִּסְא֔וֹ וַיַּעֲבֵ֥ר אַדַּרְתּ֖וֹ מֵֽעָלָ֑יו וַיְכַ֣ס שַׂ֔ק וַיֵּ֖שֶׁב עַל־הָאֵֽפֶר׃	
	[7] וַיַּזְעֵ֗ק וַיֹּ֙אמֶר֙ בְּנִֽינְוֵ֔ה מִטַּ֧עַם הַמֶּ֛לֶךְ וּגְדֹלָ֖יו לֵאמֹ֑ר הָאָדָ֨ם וְהַבְּהֵמָ֜ה הַבָּקָ֣ר וְהַצֹּ֗אן אַל־	

greatest to the least of them.

⁶ When the word reached the king of Nineveh, he arose from his throne, laid aside his robe from him, covered *himself* with sackcloth and sat on the ashes.

⁷ He issued a proclamation and it said, "In Nineveh by the decree of the king and his nobles: Do not let man, beast, herd, or flock taste a thing. Do not let them eat or drink water.

⁸ "But both man and beast must be covered with sackcloth; and let men call on God earnestly that each may turn from his wicked way and from the violence which is in his hands.

⁹ "Who knows, God may turn and relent and withdraw His burning anger so that we will not perish."

¹⁰ When God saw their deeds, that they turned from

יִטְעֲמוּ מְאוּמָה אַל־יִרְעוּ וּמַיִם אַל־יִשְׁתּוּ׃

⁸ וְיִתְכַּסּוּ שַׂקִּים הָאָדָם וְהַבְּהֵמָה וְיִקְרְאוּ אֶל־אֱלֹהִים בְּחָזְקָה וְיָשֻׁבוּ אִישׁ מִדַּרְכּוֹ הָרָעָה וּמִן־הֶחָמָס אֲשֶׁר בְּכַפֵּיהֶם׃

⁹ מִי־יוֹדֵעַ יָשׁוּב וְנִחַם הָאֱלֹהִים וְשָׁב מֵחֲרוֹן אַפּוֹ וְלֹא נֹאבֵד׃

¹⁰ וַיַּרְא הָאֱלֹהִים אֶת־מַעֲשֵׂיהֶם כִּי־שָׁבוּ מִדַּרְכָּם הָרָעָה וַיִּנָּחֶם הָאֱלֹהִים עַל־הָרָעָה אֲשֶׁר־דִּבֶּר לַעֲשׂוֹת־לָהֶם וְלֹא עָשָׂה׃

of them to the least of them.

⁶ And the word reached the king of Nineve, and he arose from off his throne, and took off his raiment from him, and put on sackcloth, and sat on ashes.

⁷ And proclamation was made, and the king commanded it in Nineve an by his great men, saying, Let not men, or cattle, or oxen, or sheep, taste *any thing*, nor feed, nor drink water.

⁸ So men and cattle were clothed with sackcloths, and cried earnestly to God; and they turned every one from their evil way, and from the iniquity that was in their hands, saying,

⁹ Who knows if God will repent, and turn from his fierce anger, and *so* we shall not perish?

¹⁰ And God saw their works, that they turned from their

their wicked way, then God relented concerning the calamity which He had declared He would bring upon them. And He did not do *it*.		evil ways; and God repented of the evil which he had said he would do to them; and he did *it* not.

Process of Discovery

Linguistics Section

Linguistic Structure

[Action] [1] Now the word of the LORD came to Jonah the second time, saying, [2] "Arise, go to Nineveh the great city and proclaim to it the proclamation which I am going to tell you."

[Reaction] [3] So Jonah arose and went to Nineveh according to the word of the LORD. Now Nineveh was an exceedingly great city, a three days' walk. [4] Then Jonah began to go through the city one day's walk; and he cried out and said, "Yet forty days and Nineveh will be overthrown."

[Action] [5] Then the people of Nineveh believed in God; and they called a fast and put on sackcloth from the greatest to the least of them.

[Continuing Action] [6] When the word reached the king of Nineveh, he arose from his throne, laid aside his robe from him, covered *himself* with sackcloth and sat on the ashes. [7] He issued a proclamation and it said, "In Nineveh by the decree of the king and his nobles: Do not let man, beast, herd, or flock taste a thing. Do not let them eat or drink water.

[Continuing Action] [8] "But both man and beast must be covered with sackcloth; and let men call on God earnestly that each may turn from his wicked way and from the violence which is in his hands.

[Anticipated reaction][9] "Who knows, God may turn and relent and withdraw His burning anger so that we will not perish."

[Reaction] [10] When God saw their deeds, that they turned from their wicked way, then God relented concerning the calamity which He had declared He would bring upon them. And He did not do *it*.

Discussion

This chapter consists of two actions and two reactions. The first action was the LORD instructing Jonah to go to Ninevah and give them the message of the need for their repentance. The second action is that the people repented, which eventually extended to the king. The king of Ninevah hoped that the LORD would forgive them.

Questioning the Passage

1. Why is Ninevah called the great city? (v. 2)

   The city of Ninevah was considered great because of the size of the city. In ancient days it was difficult to have a large city unless there was plenty of water and land available.

2. What is the significance of it being a three day walk for Jonah to get to Ninevah? (v. 3)

   The Talmud in Pesachim 93b estimates that a human can walk 10 parsas a day which is approximately 26 miles. Therefore, Jonah was 78 miles from the city.[19]

3. Why was the city of Ninevah called an exceeding great city? (v. 3)

   הָיְתָה עִיר־גְּדוֹלָהֹ לֵאלֹהִים (Jon. 3:3 WTT)

   "The translation *enormously great* follows Radak, who explains that when Scriptures wishes to emphasize size or importance, it idiomatically attaches God's name to the noun."[20] The word *El* or *Elohim* are used, not the actual name of God.

---

[19] Scherman, Nosson, and Meir Zlotowitz. "Chapter 3. Jonah" In *Jonah: The Later Prophets with a Commentary Antholigized from the Rabbinic Writings*. Brooklyn, N.Y: Mesorah Publications, 2014. p. 232.

[20] IBID, p. 233.

4. What is the significance that Ninevah was a one day walk in size? (v. 4)

This tells us that Ninevah could have been a city of 26 miles in diameter. It was a huge city which corresponds to the language of it being an enormous city. This conclusion comes from reading verse four that it took Jonah one day to walk through the city.

Main/Center Point

Jonah had decided to follow the Word of the LORD. He goes to the city of Ninevah and was probably shocked to see the people mourning for their sins. The sackcloth and fasting are a sign of repentance. When the King of Ninevah heard the words of Jonah and his people were in repentance, he joined them. The King must have heard Jonah's word through his advisor because the Bible does not say Jonah ever met the King.

People's names

1. יוֹנָה *Yonah* (402a) **Meaning:** an Israeli prophet

Name of places

1. נִינְוֵה *Nineveh* **Meaning:** capital of Assyria

Scripture cross references

Verse 4   Mat 12:41; Luk 11:32

Verse 5   Dan 9:3; Joe 1:14

Verse 6   Est 4:1-4; Jer 6:26; Eze 27:30, Eze 27:3

Verse 7   2Ch 20:3; Ezr 8:21;

Verse 8   Psalm 130:1; 2Ch 20:3; Ezr 8:21;

Verse 9   2Sa 12:22; Joe 2:14

Culture Section

Questioning the Passage

1. What is the cultural significance of sack cloth? (v. 5)

    Sack cloth and fasting is a sign of repentance. Sack cloth were garments made of goat hair. Over the years sack cloth became the name of clothing one wore when in mourning

2. What is the cultural significance that the king rose from his throne? (v. 6)

    The king rising from his throne is a sign of reverence to the LORD.

3. What is the cultural significance that the king issued a decree? (v. 7)

    The decree of the king was the king showing his people his agreement with the decision to repent and believe in the LORD. It is interesting that in this case the King was willing to follow the will of his people.

Cultural Echoes

The number 40: 40 days of rain with Noah, 40 years of Israel in the desert, Isaac was 40 years old when he married Rebekah, Esau was 40 years old when he married, Jacob presented 40 cows to Esau, 40 days to embalm Jacob when he died in Egypt, Moses was on Mt. Sinai for 40 days, the spies Moses sent into Caanan were there for 40 days, Joshua was 40 years old when Moses sent him as a spy into Caanan, forty year cycles in Judges, and a lot more.

Culture and Linguistics Section

Discussion

What is interesting is that the name of the LORD is not mentioned in this chapter. Elohim is used in the verses that speak about the people of Nineveh. The cultural understanding is that the name of the LORD is only for the Hebrews is shown here.

Thoughts

From the point of view that the book of Jonah is a prophecy, a problem occurs because history tells us that the Ninevites did not repent and when the Assyrian empire rose, with Nineveh being its capital, the people treated their enemies horribly. So many lives would have been spared from torture had the Assyrian empire never occurred. But it did occur. Therefore, another way to view the book of Jonah is to see it as a fictional book where the LORD allowed non-Hebrews to receive salvation if they repented of their evil and sins. Since the people of Israel believed for quite some time that the LORD was their God and only their God, the book of Jonah had to be a shock. In the understanding of the evolution of monotheism, Israel did not show signs of monotheism, one God for all people, until the book of Jonah was written. In this chapter we read that the LORD is God of all people.

New American Standard 1995	Hebrew	Septuagint
[1]But it greatly displeased Jonah and he became angry. 2 He prayed to the LORD and said, "Please LORD, was not this what I said while I was still in my *own* country? Therefore in order to forestall this I fled to Tarshish, for I knew that You are a gracious and compassionate God, slow to anger and abundant in lovingkindness, and one who relents concerning calamity. 3 "Therefore now, O LORD, please take my life from me, for death is better to me than life." 4 The LORD said, "Do you have good reason to be angry?" 5 Then Jonah went out	‫וַיֵּרַע אֶל־יוֹנָה רָעָה גְדוֹלָה‬[1]‫וַיִּחַר לוֹ:‬ ‫וַיִּתְפַּלֵּל אֶל־יְהוָֹה‬[2] ‫וַיֹּאמַר אָנָּה יְהוָֹה הֲלוֹא־זֶה דְבָרִי עַד־הֱיוֹתִי עַל־אַדְמָתִי עַל־כֵּן קִדַּמְתִּי לִבְרֹחַ תַּרְשִׁישָׁה כִּי יָדַעְתִּי כִּי אַתָּה אֵל־חַנּוּן וְרַחוּם אֶרֶךְ אַפַּיִם וְרַב־חֶסֶד וְנִחָם עַל־הָרָעָה:‬ ‫וְעַתָּה יְהוָֹה קַח־נָא אֶת־נַפְשִׁי‬[3]‫מִמֶּנִּי כִּי טוֹב מוֹתִי מֵחַיָּי: ס‬ ‫וַיֹּאמֶר יְהוָֹה הַהֵיטֵב חָרָה‬[4]‫לָךְ:‬ ‫וַיֵּצֵא יוֹנָה מִן־הָעִיר וַיֵּשֶׁב‬[5]‫מִקֶּדֶם לָעִיר וַיַּעַשׂ לוֹ שָׁם סֻכָּה וַיֵּשֶׁב תַּחְתֶּיהָ בַּצֵּל עַד אֲשֶׁר יִרְאֶה מַה־יִּהְיֶה בָּעִיר:‬ ‫וַיְמַן יְהוָֹה־אֱלֹהִים קִיקָיוֹן‬[6]‫וַיַּעַל מֵעַל לְיוֹנָה לִהְיוֹת צֵל עַל־רֹאשׁוֹ לְהַצִּיל לוֹ מֵרָעָתוֹ וַיִּשְׂמַח יוֹנָה עַל־הַקִּיקָיוֹן שִׂמְחָה גְדוֹלָה:‬ ‫וַיְמַן הָאֱלֹהִים תּוֹלַעַת בַּעֲלוֹת‬[7]	But Jonas was very deeply grieved, and he was confounded. 2 And he prayed to the Lord, and said, O Lord, were not these my words when I was yet in my land? therefore I made haste to flee to Tharsis; because I knew that thou are merciful and compassionate, long-suffering, and abundant in kindness, and repentest of evil. 3 And now, Lord God, take my life from me; for *it is* better for me to die than to live. 4 And the Lord said to Jonas, Art thou very much grieved? 5 And Jonas went out from the city, and sat over against the city; and he made for himself there a booth, and he sat under it, until he should perceive what would become of the city.

New American Standard 1995	Hebrew	Septuagint

<table>
<tr>
<td>

from the city and sat east of it. There he made a shelter for himself and sat under it in the shade until he could see what would happen in the city.

⁶ So the LORD God appointed a plant and it grew up over Jonah to be a shade over his head to deliver him from his discomfort. And Jonah was extremely happy about the plant.

⁷ But God appointed a worm when dawn came the next day and it attacked the plant and it withered.

⁸ When the sun came up God appointed a scorching east wind, and the sun beat down on Jonah's head so that he became faint and begged with *all* his soul to die, saying, "Death is better

</td>
<td dir="rtl">

הַשַּׁחַר לְמׇחֳרָת וַתַּ֥ךְ אֶת־הַקִּיקָיוֹן וַיִּיבָֽשׁ׃

⁸ וַיְהִ֣י ׀ כִּזְרֹ֣חַ הַשֶּׁ֗מֶשׁ וַיְמַ֨ן אֱלֹהִ֜ים ר֤וּחַ קָדִים֙ חֲרִישִׁ֔ית וַתַּ֥ךְ הַשֶּׁ֛מֶשׁ עַל־רֹ֥אשׁ יוֹנָ֖ה וַיִּתְעַלָּ֑ף וַיִּשְׁאַ֤ל אֶת־נַפְשׁוֹ֙ לָמ֔וּת וַיֹּ֕אמֶר ט֥וֹב מוֹתִ֖י מֵחַיָּֽי׃

⁹ וַיֹּ֤אמֶר אֱלֹהִים֙ אֶל־יוֹנָ֔ה הַהֵיטֵ֥ב חָרָֽה־לְךָ֖ עַל־הַקִּֽיקָי֑וֹן וַיֹּ֕אמֶר הֵיטֵ֥ב חָֽרָה־לִ֖י עַד־מָֽוֶת׃

¹⁰ וַיֹּ֣אמֶר יְהֹוָ֔ה אַתָּ֥ה חַ֙סְתָּ֙ עַל־הַקִּ֣יקָי֔וֹן אֲשֶׁ֛ר לֹא־עָמַ֥לְתָּ בּ֖וֹ וְלֹ֣א גִדַּלְתּ֑וֹ שֶׁבִּן־לַ֥יְלָה הָיָ֖ה וּבִן־לַ֥יְלָה אָבָֽד׃

¹¹ וַאֲנִי֙ לֹ֣א אָח֔וּס עַל־נִֽינְוֵ֖ה הָעִ֣יר הַגְּדוֹלָ֑ה אֲשֶׁ֣ר יֶשׁ־בָּ֡הּ הַרְבֵּה֩ מִֽשְׁתֵּים־עֶשְׂרֵ֨ה רִבּ֜וֹ אָדָ֗ם אֲשֶׁ֤ר לֹֽא־יָדַע֙ בֵּין־יְמִינ֣וֹ לִשְׂמֹאל֔וֹ וּבְהֵמָ֖ה רַבָּֽה׃

</td>
<td>

⁶ And the Lord God commanded a gourd, and it came up over the head of Jonas, to be a shadow over his head, to shade him from his calamities: and Jonas rejoiced with great joy for the gourd.

⁷ And God commanded a worm the next morning, and it smote the gourd, and it withered away.

⁸ And it came to pass at the rising of the sun, that God commanded a burning east wind; and the sun smote on the head of Jonas, and he fainted, and despaired of his life, and said, *It is* better for me to die than to live.

⁹ And God said to Jonas, Art thou very much grieved for the gourd? And he said, I am very much grieved, even to death.

¹⁰ And the Lord said, Thou hadst pity on the gourd, for

</td>
</tr>
</table>

New American Standard 1995	Hebrew	Septuagint
to me than life." 9 Then God said to Jonah, "Do you have good reason to be angry about the plant?" And he said, "I have good reason to be angry, even to death." 10 Then the LORD said, "You had compassion on the plant for which you did not work and *which* you did not cause to grow, which came up overnight and perished overnight. 11 "Should I not have compassion on Nineveh, the great city in which there are more than 120,000 persons who do not know *the difference* between their right and left hand, as well as many animals?"		which thou has not suffered, neither didst thou rear it; which came up before night, and perished before *another* night: 11 and shall not I spare Nineve, the great city, in which dwell more than twelve myriads of human beings, who do not know their right hand or their left hand; and *also* much cattle?

Process of Discovery

Linguistics Section

Linguistic Structure

A [1] **[Dissatisfaction of Jonah]** But it greatly displeased Jonah and he became angry. [2] He prayed to the LORD and said, "Please LORD, was not this what I said while I was still in my *own* country? Therefore in order to forestall this I fled to Tarshish, for I knew that You are a gracious and compassionate God, slow to anger and abundant in lovingkindness, and one who relents concerning calamity. [3] "Therefore now, O LORD, please take my life from me, for death is better to me than life."

B [4] The LORD said, "**Do you have good reason to be angry?**"

C [The LORD saves] [5] Then Jonah went out from the city and sat east of it. There he made a shelter for himself and sat under it in the shade until he could see what would happen in the city. [6] So the LORD God appointed a plant and it grew up over Jonah to be a shade over his head to deliver him from his discomfort. And Jonah was extremely happy about the plant.

A' [7] **[Dissatisfaction of Jonah]** But God appointed a worm when dawn came the next day and it attacked the plant and it withered. [8] When the sun came up God appointed a scorching east wind, and the sun beat down on Jonah's head so that he became faint and begged with *all* his soul to die, saying, "Death is better to me than life."

B' [9] Then God said to Jonah, "**Do you have good reason to be angry about the plant?**" And he said, "I have good reason to be angry, even to death."

C' [The LORD saves] [10] Then the LORD said, "You had compassion on the plant for which you did not work and *which* you did not cause to grow, which came up overnight and perished overnight. [11] "Should I not have compassion on Nineveh, the great city in which there are more than 120,000 persons who do not know *the difference* between their right and left hand, as well as many animals?"

Discussion

This chapter is a chiasm of A-B-C-A'-B'-C'. The A and C blocks are repetition because of their mutual topics. Block B is a linguistic repetition.

Questioning the Passage

1. Why was Jonah angry when the people of Nineveh listened to the Word of the LORD that Jonah brought? (v. 1)

    The people of Israel did not listen to the prophets, but the people of Nineveh did. Jonah was angry because the people did what the prophet said. The people did repent. Why would these aliens listen to the LORD's Word while the LORD's people did not listen? It does appear to indicate a different level of trust and honor of the LORD, and it was not from the children of Israel.

2. What did Jonah say in "his own country?" (v. 2)

    The text does not have Jonah saying anything but rather fleeing. This verse is referring to the event of Jonah fleeing from the Word of the LORD while he was in Israel. Jonah did not want to take a prophecy to a foreign people who were probably idol worshipers.[21]

3. Why did Jonah desire death? (v. 3)

    Jonah might have known that Israel would not repent and that the Assyrians would eventually invade and destroy the ten northern tribes. Jonah preferred death rather than seeing his country destroyed and his people killed.

---

[21] Scherman, Nosson, and Meir Zlotowitz. "Chapter 3. Jonah" In *Jonah: The Later Prophets with a Commentary Antholigized from the Rabbinic Writings*. Brooklyn, N.Y: Mesorah Publications, 2014. p. 235.

4. Why did the LORD have to ask Jonah about His anger? (v. 4)

This is a rhetorical question, implying that Jonah would yet be shown that his displeasure was improper (Rashi[22]).[23]

5. Is there any significance to Jonah sitting east of the city? (v. 5)

By sitting to the east of the city the sun would be able to shine upon him. It was safer to be on the east side of the city because the city gates of ancient cities were built on the east side. The gate would have soldiers there for defense of an enemy attack.

6. What is the symbolism of the plant that grew around Jonah? (v. 6)

The plant is simply a divine gesture of the LORD to comfort Jonah in his distress.

7. Why did God take the plant away from Jonah? (v. 7)

The worm came in the morning to eat the plant just when Jonah needed it for its shade. Perhaps the LORD took the plant because it was given to him for comfort yet Jonah remained angry at the events that had taken place in the city. Was Jonah angry with himself or was he angry with his people? A prophet who cannot influence God's people but can influence the aliens is not a prophet of the LORD. This could be the reason for Jonah's distress.

The LORD has given the plant to cheer up Jonah. But Jonah did not let go of his anger. So, the LORD took the gift away.

8. What is the symbolism of the scorching east wind? (v. 8)

The wind is not a symbol, it is just an additional stress on Jonah. The sun and the wind would have made things uncomfortable for Jonah. This could be viewed as a punishment to Jonah for his attitude towards what the LORD wanted done. If one is truly a servant

---

[22] French commentator on Bible and Talmud; born at Troyes in 1040; died there July 13, 1105. His fame has made him the subject of many legends. Source: http://jewishencyclopedia.com

[23] IBID. p. 235

of the LORD then one should not question how God works.

9. What is the comparison of Jonah's compassion for the plant and God's compassion for Nineveh? (v. 10 & 11)

Jonah had compassion for the plant that he did not plant nor cultivate. God was saying that He created the people of Nineveh and that He had compassion for them. This is a further example of how the Israelites needed to come to understand monotheism. The LORD was the God of all people. By sparing the people from death because of their evil ways, thus offering salvation, the LORD shows the Hebrews about the extent of the power of the LORD.

People's names

1. יוֹנָה *Yonah* **Meaning:** an Israeli prophet

Name of places

1. נִינְוֵה *Nineveh* **Meaning:** capital of Assyria

Word Study

1. סֻכָּה *sukkah* **Meaning:** *a thicket, booth*

   NAU **Leviticus 23:34** "Speak to the sons of Israel, saying, 'On the fifteenth of this seventh month is the Feast of **Booths** for seven days to the LORD. (Lev. 23:34 NAU)

   NAU **2 Samuel 11:11** Uriah said to David, "The ark and Israel and Judah are staying in temporary **shelters**, and my LORD Joab and the servants of my LORD are camping in the open field. Shall I then go to my house to eat and to drink and to lie with my wife? By your life and the life of your soul, I will not do this thing." (2 Sam. 11:11 NAU)

   NAU **2 Samuel 22:12** "And He made darkness **canopies** around Him, A mass of waters, thick clouds of the sky. (2 Sam. 22:12 NAU)

^{NAU} **1 Kings 20:12** When *Ben-hadad* heard this message, as he was drinking with the kings in the temporary **shelters**, he said to his servants, "Station *yourselves.*" So they stationed *themselves* against the city. (1 Ki. 20:12 NAU)

Conclusion

Sukkah is used in two manners in the Scripture. As the verses above indicate the word means "shelter." Jonah built himself a shelter because he could not find a place to sleep. Refer to the cultural section for more information. Jonah had traversed the city warning the people about the upcoming doom. It is possible that he did not want to stay in the city that evening. Therefore, since he slept that evening outside the city, to the east of the city, he needed to build himself a shelter.

^{NAU} **Leviticus 23:34** "Speak to the sons of Israel, saying, 'On the fifteenth of this seventh month is the Feast of Booths for seven days to the LORD. (Lev. 23:34 NAU)

This verse from Leviticus is one of many which refers to the Feast of Booths (Sukkot) in which the Hebrews built *Sukkot,* shelters out in the fields during the fall harvest. There is a debate as to whether or the reference about Sukkot is about the Festival or some other concern. Connecting the Jonah Sukkot would create an interesting midrash interpretation.

Scripture cross references

Verse 1 Mat 20:15; Luk 15:28

Verse 3   1Ki 19:4; Job 6:8, Job 6:9; Job 7:15, Job 7:16; Ecc 7:1

Verse 5 1Ki 19:9, 1Ki 19:13

Verse 8 Eze 19:12; Hos 13:15; Psa 121:6; Isa 49:10

Culture Section

Discussion

When visitors came to a city and could not find a place to sleep they would go outside of the city and sleep under a tree. Jonah went outside the city to sleep that night. He created a shelter and the LORD provided a tree for him to sleep under.[24]

Questioning the Passage

1. What does it mean not to know the difference between the right and left hand? (v. 11)

This is a Semitic idiom which means the person is too young to discern between good and evil. The left hand is evil while the right hand is good.[25]

2. What is the reference to the animals in verse ten?

"This figuratively refers to the adults who had beastlike sensibilities, inasmuch as they do not know their Creator (Rashi). Alternatively, and many animals, literally. Certainly they are innocent and deserving of compassion, especially since they are many (Radak)."[26]

Thoughts

Jonah's anger with what happened in Nineveh is directed toward himself as a prophet because he knew that Israel would not listen to him yet an enemy of Israel did. It must have been frustrating to think that the people of the LORD would not accept the salvation the LORD offered but the foreigners did. Eventually the Assyrians destroyed the Northern Kingdom after they were warned by numerous prophets.

The other area to consider is monotheism. It was the LORD who offered salvation to the people of Nineveh. Ancient people believed that their gods were their gods alone. The

---

[24] Errico, Rocco A., and George M. Lamsa. *Aramaic Light on Ezekiel, Daniel, and the Minor Prophets: A Commentary Based on the Aramaic Language and Ancient Near Eastern Customs.* p. 165.

[25] IBID. p 165.

[26] Scherman, Nosson, and Meir Zlotowitz. "Chapter 3. Jonah" In *Jonah: The Later Prophets with a Commentary Antholigized from the Rabbinic Writings.* Brooklyn, N.Y: Mesorah Publications, 2014. p. 237.

Hebrews would have had the same attitude. The LORD was the creator of Heaven and Earth but was not the God of all people. It is clear in the Jonah story that the LORD was the God of all people because of the salvation to Nineveh. The development of monotheism would have taken centuries to develop and for the people to accept. So, the book of Jonah serves several purposes. Monotheism is one, salvation for all people, and when God wants you for a task it is best to do it.

Works Cited

Bowker, John. 2005. "Isaac Abravanel." In *The Concise Oxford Dictionary of World Religions*. Oxford: England: Oxford University Press.

Errico, Rocco and George Lamsa. 2012. *Aramaic Light on Ezekiel, Daniel and the Minor Prophets. A commentary based on the Aramaic Near Eastern Customs. Smyna, Georgia: Noohra Foundation*

http://jewishencyclopedia.com – The Jewish Encyclopedia

Scherman, Nosson, Meir Zlotowitz, Sheah Brander, and Menachem Davis. 2014. *The Prophets: The Later Prophets with a Commentary Anthologized from the Rabbinical Writings*. Brooklyn, NY: Mesorah Publications.

.